"$\mathscr{T}$ think I am the happiest missionary in the world. The sacrifice of my health which God has been pleased to accept in allowing my ministry among the lepers to bear a little fruit seems after all to be a light and even pleasant burden."

– FATHER JOSEPH DAMIEN deVEUSTER, KALAWAO 1887,

THE LANDS OF
Father Damien

KALAUPAPA   MOLOKAI   HAWAII

ACKNOWLEDGEMENTS:

The author wishes to express his sincere gratitude to the following organizations and individuals who have made this publication possible. Damien Museum and Archives, and its director, Irene Letoto; Patrick Downes, Editor, *Hawaii Catholic Herald*; Patrick Boland, Damien Historian; Hawaii State Archives; Hawaii State Department of Health; former and current Kalaupapa Settlement Administrators; U.S. National Parks Service; and Ellen Osborne of Mapulehu, Molokai. Above all else, a heartfelt thanks to the many former patients, residents and staff of the Kalaupapa Settlement, both living and deceased, whom the author has called friends for the past 35 years.

ABOUT THE AUTHOR:

Born and raised of German ancestry in the farm and ranching country of central Texas, the author received his formal education at Sam Houston State University, majoring in Business Administration and History. He is a Federal Aviation Administration certified Airline Transport Pilot in both single and multi-engine aircraft, a commercial helicopter pilot, and a Certified Flight Instructor in both single and multi-engine jet and propeller powered fixed-wing aircraft and helicopters.

During his diversified flying career, Brocker has logged over 13,000 hours of flight time world-wide, which included pilot training for Central and South American governments as well as several years in the capacity of an airport manager. With extensive flying throughout the South Pacific, he has made hundreds of commercial flights in and out of the small Kalaupapa Airport on Molokai. Jim also guided visitors on the Kalaupapa Peninsula before the segregation ban was lifted in 1969, which allowed former patients to come into contact with visitors from the outside.

Calling Hawaii his home since the 1960s, Brocker moved from Honolulu to the Island of Molokai in the late 1970s, and after a time put aside his flying career to establish several corporations in the retail and wholesale trades. Among his hobbies are raising rare and exotic tropical parrots, photography, horticulture, scuba diving and fishing. He has also authored *A Portrait of Molokai* which takes a step-by-step journey around the island, describing the history and local culture of Molokai.

Jim Brocker at the Kalaupapa Airport during the 1960s.

PHOTOGRAPHY & ARTWORK:

Book format, design and color photographs by James H. Brocker. Sepia and black and white photographs were collected and reproduced by the same, being gathered as a result of the generous permission of those noted; these photographs remain the property of their respective owners listed below:

Damien Museum and Archives
Hawaii State Archives
Hawaii Catholic Herald & Lisa Benoit
Department of the Interior, State of Hawaii

Front Cover Artwork: Maria Thompson
Front Cover Photo: Damien Museum and Archives

Inside Front Cover: Our Lady of Peace Church, Honolulu

Inside Title Page Drawing: Maria Thompson
    - consent from Walter Josten & Sue Dawe

Inside Back Cover Photo: Papaloa, Kalaupapa

Back Cover Artwork: Maria Thompson

Copyright © 1997 by James H. Brocker

Distributor: James H. Brocker
P.O. Box 576
Kaunakakai, Molokai, Hawaii 96748-0576
(808) 553-5926

Publisher: James H. Brocker

UPC # 79437300000
ISBN 0-9642197-3-5

First Printing Standard Edition, 1998
Limited Edition, 1998

Printed in Hong Kong

TABLE OF CONTENTS

FOREWORD

Many an idea for a book as the first sentence begins is far different when the last paragraph is completed and is finally put on the printer's desk. It was no exception with this publication. The main purpose for its creation is to preserve in photographs a testimony to the people who lived, died, and were for the most part forgotten on a little parcel of land in the middle of the Pacific Ocean.

Before journeying any farther between the covers of this book, the author would like to make two important facts known to the reader. For thousands of years the word leper has been used throughout the world when referring to a person carrying the leprosy bacteria. Officially adopted in Hawaii in 1981, the medical word for leprosy is now Hansen's Disease. It is the desire of the medical profession as well as those living at Kalaupapa, correctly referred to as former patients, that the disease be referred to as such. The author agrees with this terminology, except when used within a historical time frame or in a direct quote in this book.

To term someone a leper or having leprosy is to brand a person with an illness that was beyond their control, much as AIDS is presently, and should be avoided because of its sinister overtones. Over time, Hansen's Disease has been feared and misunder-

Charles Warren Stoddard, who visited Father Damien in 1884, described ascending the long trail from Kalaupapa to Topside Molokai: "It was every man for himself... there was one terrible bit of wall-like cliff that was almost perpendicular; it crumbled as we clung to it like cats; and when I looked below to find footing, I discovered that the rock upon which I was stretched in agony of suspense was apparently overhanging the sea...then I nearly fell from sheer fright...I tried to forget that I was suspended in mid-air by my eyelids, with nothing but sole-leather between me and a thousand feet of space, with certain death at the lower end of it. We were rained upon and shined upon, covered with dust and debris, and when we reached the top of the pali I was dizzy and parched with thirst...we made it in two hours and forty minutes, with my heart knocking wildly at my ribs all the way up."

stood, mainly from the lack of knowledge about it. Because of the medical ignorance as to how it was transmitted, its stages of advancement or what remedies to pursue to stop it, the people afflicted were cast aside from society and forced to live their lives in subhuman existence at the edge of civilization. With the discovery of the leprosy bacillus by Dr. Gerhardt Henrik Armauer Hansen of Norway in 1873, the disease has been brought from the dark ages into a time of understanding and skilled medical treatment.

Now, we know that the bacteria alone does not kill a person, but weakens their immune system, leaving them more sensitive to contracting other infections which in turn may lead to their death. There are several forms of the disease; to most people, however, they are presently broadly grouped together and are generally referred to simply as Hansen's Disease. At its onset, white or reddish spots appear on the skin with a lack of sweat around them, often accompanied with an itching or tingling sensation in the legs, arms or hands. Beyond these symptoms, the nerves begin to be affected and the loss of feeling in certain areas begin. As the nerves start dying, the muscles start to weaken, often leaving the hands and feet crippled and turning inward. Depending upon the person's resistance to disease, damage to the eyes, nasal and throat passages may occur, as well as swelling sores or ulcers which increase in number and size as time goes on. The disease is far less infectious as it was once believed. It takes a relatively long time in close association with an untreated carrier for the bacteria to be passed to another person.

After Dr. Hansen's discovery of the bacillus, the first major breakthrough came in 1946 with the discovery of a sulfone-based drug named Dapsone. While it was not a cure for the disease, it did ease the symptoms. If the drug were discontinued for any reason, the bacteria would again become active and subsequently much harder to treat the second time around. As the years rolled by and medical technology advanced, Dapsone was replaced by several more powerful drugs which, when taken under very strict conditions, attacked the disease with such force that it was rendered noncontagious within a few weeks. Today, after receiving such treatment, a person is able to live out their life as normally as someone who has never been infected with the bacteria in the first place.

Although Hansen's Disease is seldom thought of in this day of high-technology, there are an estimated 10 to 12 million people throughout the world who have been infected. A number of countries where these people reside maintain a registry of those who have the disease, in an effort to ensure that it is treated properly and kept from spreading. Primarily due to the fact that many of those afflicted live in remote and uncontrollable regions of the earth, only a little over 5 million people have registered for treatment with the appropriate authorities.

In 1949 the Department of Health decided that the distance and isolation of the Kalaupapa Settlement from resources abundant on Oahu was becoming too great for the continued shipment of patients on a full-scale basis to Molokai. As a result, the department opened a new facility called Hale Mohalu in Pearl City near Honolulu, for those with Hansen's Disease. With its opening, no longer was Kalaupapa to be the hub of activities dealing with the disease, and its importance as a center for treatment and isolation began to wane. This paved the way for the last patients, at their request, to be allowed to reside at Kalaupapa Peninsula's rocky shores.

As the fear of Hansen's Disease dissolved and corrective medicine became better and more available to treat the out-patients, the need for isolation and segregation became unwarranted. As it did, the barriers that separated the patients from non-patients began to crumble. In 1969 the Department of Health reviewed their 104-year-old policy regarding segregation and decided that it was antiquated and no longer necessary. The laws were repealed. Down came the physical divisions which had held the people of the peninsula captive for so long. The peninsula's old warning signs and fences that kept those with Hansen's Disease apart from the workers and visitors were removed. No longer was the outgoing mail fumigated or the former patients treated as unequals - they were free at last! The people could travel and visit family and friends anywhere in the state they wished. For that matter, they were free to go to any one of the four corners of the earth if they

so desired. There were some who moved, but their numbers were few. The majority stayed where they were, at home on the shores of the Kalaupapa Peninsula.

The Kalaupapa Peninsula, composed of the three districts of Kalawao, Makanalua and Kalaupapa, holds vast historical significance, the result of its 130 years as a Hansen's Disease settlement and the nearly 1,000 years of habitation by natives before it became a place of banishment. The peninsula is a virtual gold mine of untouched and virgin archaeological sites; this offers valuable insights into the culture and customs which long ago vanished.

In 1973 the Congress of the United States introduced a bill declaring the Kalaupapa Peninsula an historical site. In 1980, President Carter signed into law the setting aside of 10,726 acres that were to be known as the Kalaupapa National Park. Included in this figure were 2,000 acres of adjacent lands and valleys to the south, as well as waters surrounding the peninsula.

Today this area is under joint control of both the State of Hawaii Department of Health and the United States National Park System. Under their careful jurisdiction, a limited number of controlled visits are allowed into the settlement each day to tour selected locations. There never seems to be a problem with exceeding the quota of 100 visitors per day, however, as on most days there are hardly more than several dozen people that set foot in Kalaupapa to take the special tour.

The peninsula and its neighboring lands are governed by special regulations and enforceable laws concerning all visits. Entries are allowed by advance permit only, and no permits are issued to anyone under 16 years of age, regardless of the circumstances. Once within the boundaries of the park, for the privacy and protection of the former patients and for the preservation of archaeological sites, at no time is anyone allowed to wander around the areas of the peninsula unchaperoned. Hawaii statutes also prohibit photographing or filming any resident without their prior written consent. There is no camping allowed, nor are there any food services available. All visitors on the tour must be out of the area before sunset. In addition, no hunting, fishing or gathering of any object is allowed. A $1,000 fine per incident may be levied on any individual who violates these state and federal laws.

Arrangements for conducted tours of the settlement can be made by writing to Kalaupapa Historical

The Kalaupapa Settlement and Peninsula from the Palaau State Park lookout.

Park, Kalaupapa, Hawaii, 96742. To enter the Kalaupapa National Park, a visitor with the required permit can use any one of three modes of transportation, or a combination thereof. From the Palaau State Park in Kalae, one is able to walk down the old trail as did the ancient Hawaiians and Father Damien himself. Maintained by the Parks Department, the trail is in far better condition today than it was during the earlier periods of its history, although it is still very narrow and steep. There are also guided mule rides down the same trail which can be used to relieve the wear and tear on one's legs by directing it to another spot.

For the less adventurous, there is a seven-minute flight from Molokai's Hoolehua Airport to Kalaupapa. The plane ride allows its passengers to have a brief scan of the entire northern coastline before arriving in a toe-gripping landing. Like the condition of the trail, the short Kalaupapa runway is not too bad. Even with the improvements, however, only the smallest commuter airplanes are used to bring visitors and supplies, such as the daily newspaper, mail and bags of fresh poi, to Kalaupapa.

A person wanting to take the tour can also mix and match their trips in and out off the Kalaupapa Settlement. It is possible to walk or ride down and fly back up or do it completely in reverse. To walk down the trail will take about one-and-a-half hours to reach the bottom; walking up from below, plan on an additional half-hour to the time it took to get down. On the mules, it will take about an hour each way. All three modes of traveling offer a breathtaking and magnificent view of the spectacular cliffs with the settlement nestled below.

Regardless of how you get there, to visit Kalaupapa and Kalawao today is truly a humbling experience that leaves a person with mixed emotions almost immediately as they say good-bye to the little peninsula. Even though they might not be aware of it as they depart, each of them carries a little part of the tragedy that took place on this land tucked away in a remote part of their mind or heart. Returning to the world of traffic jams, movie theaters and shopping malls, none who visit here leave with any lightheartedness unless it is from the fact they know that things today at Kalaupapa, as well as the world-over, are far different for people with Hansen's Disease, and they have just walked upon the very grounds where the many who had endured so much walked before them.

With this last thought, let us begin our story, *The Lands of Father Damien.*

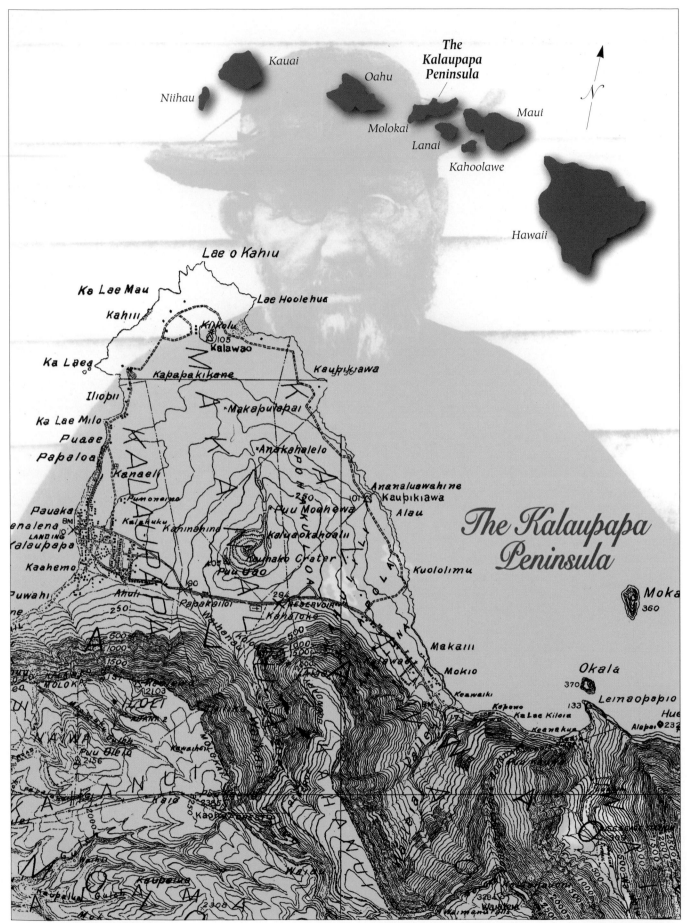

Niihau

Kauai

Oahu

The Kalaupapa Peninsula

Molokai

Maui

Lanai

Kahoolawe

N

Hawaii

Lae o Kahiu

Ka Lae Mau

Lae Hoolehua

Kahiii

Kikolu

105

Kalawao

Ka Laea

Kapapakikane

Kaupikiawa

Iliopii

Makapulapai

Ka Lae Milo

Anakahalelo

Puaae

Ananaluawahine

Papaloa

Kaupikiawa

Kanaeli

250

Alau

Pumoneina

Puu Moehewa

101

Pauaka
enalena

Kalaupapa

Kalahuku

Kahinahina

Kaluaokahoalii

The Kalaupapa

Ahuli

Kauhako Crater

Peninsula

Kaahemo

Puu Uao

Kuololimu

90

Moka

Puwahi

Ahuli

250

Rapakailoi

Kahaloko

360

500

600
1000

Makaili

Okalá

1500

1000
1500

Mokio

370

Leinaopapio

MOLOKAI

2103

800

Keawaiki

133

Hue

BM

Kopono

Ka Lae Kiloia

Alapai 232

NA WA

Puu Olele
2156

Keanakua

Kaio

336

Kaoha

378

Waikolu
Waimanu Falls

250

Kaupeelua

2308

Mo

THE SANDWICH ISLANDS

In the middle of the vast Pacific Ocean, thousands of miles from any major continent, lies a string of small, emerald-hued islands whose peaks thrust upward from fathomless, cobalt waters. The archipelago consists of 8 major islands and numerous others, settled only by seals, sea birds and turtles, with a sprinkling of tall, waving coconut trees. The major islands named in order of their alignment from east to west are: Hawaii, Maui, Kahoolawe, Molokai, Lanai, Oahu, Kauai and Niihau. Once called the Sandwich Islands, the chain was named in 1778 by its discoverer, Captain James Cook. In the latter part of the Nineteenth Century, however, the name was replaced with Hawaii to identify the entire archipelago.

It is on one of these tiny Islands of Hawaii that our story of great suffering and perseverance unfolds. The island is called Molokai and lies in an east-west direction, between the islands of Oahu, 26 miles to the west, and Maui, 8 miles to the east. Molokai is some 2,200 miles from the west coast of the United States. The island is 37 miles long and never more than 10 miles wide at any given point; with 88 miles of coastal shoreline, of which 14 miles contain some of the highest sea cliffs in the world, Molokai's total land area of 261 square miles qualifies the Island as the fifth largest in the Hawaiian Archipelago.

Over the ages, Molokai's population has changed very little when compared to the other inhabited islands in the chain. Settled since about 600 A.D., her population seems to hover in one spot and never gets over the 10,000 mark. In 1836, Molokai's population was reported by *The Missionary Herald* of Honolulu as being 8,700 people; of these, 2,700 lived on or within a few miles of the Kalaupapa Peninsula. In the 1920s, the entire island's population dropped to 1,120 people; presently, it is about 7,000 people.

The creation of Molokai was the result of three separate volcanoes as they pushed molten lava from the ocean's floor. They were located where the island's West End, East End and the Kalaupapa Peninsula are today. Over the ages, lava flows from the 2 larger volcanic mountains to the east and west formed a plain between them; as a result, one large island was created. The third volcanic eruption, only one-half a million years old and the smallest of the three, formed a 2 1/4 mile wide area of land, the Kalaupapa Peninsula. The brief activity of its volcano, Kauhako, did not allow the lava to reach the height above sea level that its two older and bigger sisters attained. Rather than pushing upward, it spread its mass outward to rise just a little more than 400 feet above the violent waters surrounding it. Eons ago, the northern shore of Molokai crumbled and fell into the ocean, creating steep and unscalable cliffs rising hundreds of feet above the ocean. During its later eruption, Kauhako effectively welded itself to this cliff, thereby becoming a permanent part of the entire island. The Kalaupapa Peninsula points the tip and two of its sides directly into the powerful winds and waves of the Pacific. As a result of exposure to these salty northeast tradewinds roaring across its harsh surface, the low-lying land mass was bare of trees and vegetation for most of history. The fact that it is surrounded by a deep, furious ocean on three sides, framed with razor-sharp lava rocks at water's edge and blocked by high cliffs on the fourth side make the Kalaupapa Peninsula a natural prison. Indeed, the peninsula is one of the most isolated, remote and primeval places in all Hawaii.

The peninsula is divided into three districts: Kalawao, whose shores are craggy and weather-beaten to the east; Kalaupapa, placid and accessible by boat to the west; and Makanalua, with the dormant volcano Kauhako and surrounding land separating the former two. Today, although the peninsula is comprised of these separate land divisions, all are simply refered to by most as Kalaupapa, without regard to the distinct and separate districts. For the purpose of this book, and historical references, however, each district will be referred to by its proper name.

For centuries the only way to get from sea level at Kalaupapa to the top of the high cliffs has been a narrow path chiseled into the side of the cliff's wall. It starts near Awahua Bay and ascends to the district known as Kalae, which today is referred to as Topside Molokai. The trail is nearly perpendicular, over 3 miles long and 1,600 feet in elevation. Along its course are 26 switchbacks that corkscrew in and out of the various canyons and ravines.

It was adjacent to the base of this trail that for over 900 years there existed an isolated settlement of Islanders who, without interference from the outside world, lived their lives in tranquility and harmony with themselves and their aina, land. The people of this village called Kalaupapa quietly went about their unhurried and simple life, fishing the rough, surrounding oceans by outrigger canoe with nets and spears. They also farmed the land, coaxing the harsh

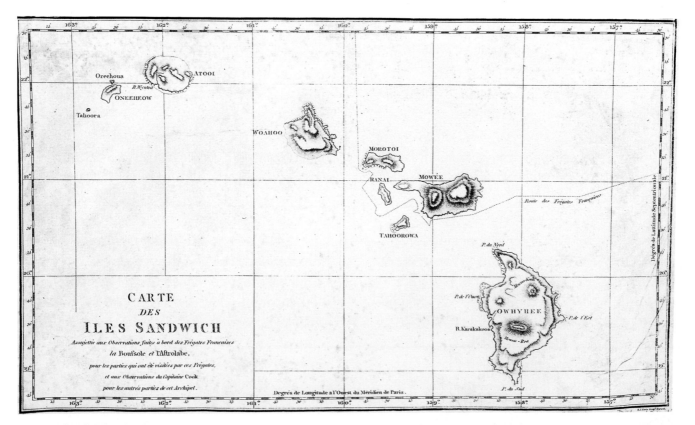

The Sandwich Islands, drawn by J.F. de LaPerouse in 1786 while on the ship Boutsole. Notice how the spelling of the recently discovered archipelago, such as Mowee for Maui and Woahoo for Oahu, was made in relation to the sounds produced by the speech of the natives, who had no written language. HAWAII STATE ARCHIVES

volcanic soil into giving them sweet potatoes, onions and, on a limited scale, taro. With the vines of the sweet potato, their main vegetable, they fed their pigs, which in turn they used to barter with other villagers in the nearby eastern valleys.

While the rest of the peninsula was not largely settled, it was traveled much and used extensively. The entire area is divided by low rock walls that continue for mile after mile, creating thousands of small lots of every imaginable shape. With no written history of the people who built them, the theory is that they were constructed as pens for raising pigs, as windbreaks for growing crops and possibly as property boundaries and land divisions.

Numerous camp sites left from the old days are visible today, scattered at spots along the peninsula's coastline. Blended in the areas can be found fishing shrines, made of stones in circular or square-shaped platforms. The early Hawaiians built these structures to make offerings for their safety while fishing in the turbulent waters that surrounded the peninsula. There are also lava tubes and caves which were not only used as temporary shelters in bad weather or when a war was raging, but also as permanent homes. Some of these shelters have small family shrines erected within the enclosure, where the owners made known to their gods their wishes for health, peace and prosperity. In addition to the shelters and shrines, there are twelve major stone heiau, temples, sites which were constructed before there was written history in the Islands. Built for worship and making offerings to gods whose names are unknown, they stand today as silent reminders of a culture that remains forever lost.

As the centuries turned slowly over, very little change occurred in the day-to-day lifestyle of these bronze-skinned people who called the lands of the Kalaupapa Peninsula their home. Their existence, while not easy, was good in the

sense that the sea and land gave them all that was needed to be content within their tiny universe. The atmosphere that prevailed was one typical of the Hawaiian race: tranquility and proud self-reliance filled with iron-willed determination.

In the 1860s, however, the lonely peninsula's future would be changed from an easygoing and peaceful lifestyle to one where a dark cloud of sorrow and despair cast its gloomy shadow over that small sliver of land. For a time, the entire world would close its eyes so as not to see the horrors that were held before them.

In days of old, sailing vessels carried with them an artist who was skilled enough to capture in pen and ink drawings the many things of interest which the ship passed along the way. Such was this excellent sketch of a heavily tattooed Sandwich Island dancing man by John Webber while on the ship Discovery during the third and final voyage of Capt. James Cook. HAWAII STATE ARCHIVES

In ancient times the cloud of the supernatural spirit world cast its shadow into every aspect of the Islanders' lives and set the rule for much of their day-to-day living. In the days before the white man came to their land, the people placed likenesses of their gods, such as these lava rock idols, on the altars of the temples they created. HAWAII STATE ARCHIVES

A City of Refuge, depicted here, was an area where a person who committed a crime against the laws of ancient Hawaii would be safe from punishment if they could reach the confines of the compound before being caught. Wooden idols carved from huge forest trees were placed near the entrance to stand guard and offer protection to those who sought it. Drawn by Jacques Uranie in 1819 while on the Ship Varmie, captained by Louis de Freycinet.

HAWAII STATE ARCHIVES

Native women perform a night hula for the crew of the ship Discovery. Drawn during Captain James Cook's third voyage to the South Pacific.
HAWAII STATE ARCHIVES

Three warriors of the Sandwich Islands perform a traditional feast dance to the rhythm of pounding drums. Drawn by Louis Choris in 1816 while on the Otto von Kotzebue voyage. HAWAII STATE ARCHIVES

A traditional hula is performed by the residents of a Sandwich Island village in honor of visiting dignitaries and members of a ship's crew. The dancer's movements are accompanied by five natives pounding out the rhythm on ipu, gourds. The drummers are kneeling on a handwoven lauhala mat. Drawn in 1836 by Barthelme-Lauvergue while on the ship "Bontie" captained by Auguste N. Villant. HAWAII STATE ARCHIVES

Another hula performance, this one in the presence of a local governor of the Island of Hawaii, the largest land mass in the archipelago. It seems that the second best seat and a bird's eye view of the celebration is taken by the man clinging to the tall pole. Behind the crowd is the massive volcano that gave birth to the island, Mauna Kea, White Mountain. Towering two miles into the sky, its name is derived from the fact that much of the year its peak is crowned with a layer of snow. Drawn in 1824 by an unknown artist. HAWAII STATE ARCHIVES

LEPROSY INVADES THE ARCHIPELAGO

*B*efore the arrival to the Sandwich Islands by the white man and the invasion of his tall ships to hunt the great whales of the Pacific, the native population was strong and stable. Europeans and others that sailed to these virgin lands brought with them diseases previously unheard of by the people who called the islands home. To their sandy shores and green valleys came a flood of cholera, smallpox, influenza, venereal disease, leprosy and even the common cold. As they had little or no resistance to such infections, the natives succumbed easily to the diseases that spread throughout the archipelago. It has been estimated that at the time of Captain Cook's arrival to the Sandwich Islands, the population was about 300,000. In the late 1800s, however, just over 100 years later, their numbers had declined drastically to a little over 40,000, due to the invasion of various diseases.

There has never been any proof of how or when the leprosy bacteria was brought to the Islands. Believed to have been introduced as early as 1820, it was thought to have come from far-away China. The first Chinese arrived in the Sandwich Islands in 1789 as they made their way to the United States. When the vessels that transported them returned to China, they brought with them news of the Islands and the opportunities for commerce. By 1792, a thriving trade emerged between the two lands, with the exchange of aromatic native sandalwood for brocaded cloth and other exotic imports produced in the Orient. As the number of Chinese in the archipelago grew, so did the belief that it was they who brought the leprosy

bacteria. Soon the term mai pake, the Chinese sickness, became the word of preference used to describe this disease.

The first known case of mai pake was documented in the village of Koloa on Kauai, where a woman displayed the signs of the disease in 1835. When and from whom she contracted it is unknown. The outward signs are very slow to develop, and a person may be carrying the bacteria in his body for months or years before any symptoms become visible. In the beginning, as with most diseases of epidemic proportions, it took leprosy time to spread its roots deep into the community. At first there were a few scattered cases on one island, then several more on a neighboring island, probably brought there by a nameless native visiting a relative. All too soon the small seed sprouted and began to spread its roots, growing into a massive, all-consuming trunk whose branches covered the entire island chain, casting an ominous, dark cloud under its expanse.

Leprosy took victims of all races and creeds into its ever-growing folds. It struck Hawaiians much more frequently than it did Caucasians and other races; children were more susceptible than adults, and more men than women contracted the disease by almost two to one. By the 1850s, leprosy had become a concern in the Islands; by the 1860s, that concern turned into alarm and panic as the disease rapidly advanced to epidemic proportions.

It was decided by the kingdom's Board of Health that those who contracted mai pake should at all cost be isolated from the rest of society to prevent its further spread. The board selected two sites to be used to send the growing number of persons that had the infection. On Oahu, they established the Kalihi Hospital on the outskirts of Honolulu for those people who were suspects or had less advanced cases. For those in whom the disease was more progressed and the condition considered to be without hope, it was decided to banish them from all inhabited communities in the Islands. The Board of Health chose the isolated peninsula of Kalaupapa, 50 miles away from Honolulu, as this place.

King Kamehameha V, in an effort to save the remnants of his vanishing people, signed into law an "Act to Prevent the Spread of Leprosy" on January 3, 1865. By September 20, 1865, in a land exchange with the native inhabitants, the kingdom gained control of some eight hundred acres on the Kalaupapa Peninsula in the eastern district of Kalawao.

Kalawao seemed to be ideal for banishment because of its complete isolation from other settlements and from most other people. A most pitiful place it was: for most of the year, one could not see a sunrise or sunset, and the lingering dampness made it impossible to warm one's bones throughout the long nights. The strong northeast tradewinds howled relentlessly, blasting their heavy salt-laden air across the rocky lands where no trees and very little else grew.

The government's official sign concerning leprosy was posted in every village and public place on each island, proclaiming the new law: "All lepers are required to report to the Board of Health within fourteen days from this date for inspection and final banishment to Molokai." The authorities then set out to round up anyone who was suspected of being infected with the disease. They came to their homes and families indiscriminately: the rich and the poor, the bronzed-skinned and the white-skinned, tearing family and friends apart forever.

As this news circulated throughout the Islands, it was not long before the people began to hide themselves and their loved ones from the authorities. Deep into the cane fields, remote valleys and caves they went, to escape the long arm of the law as it made its way from village to village. While this usually gave them a little more precious time to share with their families and friends, eventually most were caught and brought before the Board of Health.

Those ordered to be taken away from their loved ones lost everything in life: their wealth, their homes, their possessions, even their dignity. Friends, husbands and wives, parents and children, it made no difference. Uncountable were the broken hearts and dreams as people were forced to leave all that they had ever known and loved; they were completely separated and cut off from society. Now, another name for leprosy rose above the sound of the distant winds and crashing surf. From the despairing wails came the cries of the island people: "Mai Hookaawale," "The Separating Sickness," because it literally tore families apart.

It was one year and three days after signing the Prevention Act, on January 6, 1866, when the first group of nine men and three women left the Kalihi Station in Honolulu and sailed east for the surf-beaten rocky shore of Kalawao. This small group of sufferers who were banished to Molokai that day were the vanguard for the thousands that were to follow in the next hundred years. Shipload after shipload of those arrested and detained were brought to the docks at Honolulu and loaded aboard steamers headed for the barren plains of the Kalaupapa Peninsula. In an effort not to embarrass their families with their affliction, many of those sent away concealed their identities by changing their names. Still others were shipped off with only the name of "Man," "Woman," "Boy" or "Girl" on the records.

When they arrived at Kalawao, there was

neither a landing nor a pier for them to step on. Indeed, there were no signs of anything having come ashore at this place ever before. Once the shock of their abrupt arrival on the peninsula had worn off, the basic needs of survival became the utmost concern to the survivors. There were no shelters, nor were there stores to buy the simplest things. With no tools or materials, it was impossible to construct housing to protect them from the savage winds that constantly blew across the peninsula. There were no medicines and no doctors. There was no authority. There was nothing but emptiness surrounded by an empty land. The outcasts constructed the most basic and primitive shelters, making frameworks of branches and dead roots to which they attached clumps of wild grass. When limbs and grass could not be found, they huddled with their few belongings between the many boulders or behind the remnants of stone walls that the original settlers had erected long before. With only mildew-laden grass mats or their clothing to protect them from the elements, many became sick in their lungs, which added to their worsening problems. Death called at Kalawao daily, with hardly a soul to notice the anguished sufferers in their last tormented and agonizing hours.

Of the two settlements on the peninsula, Kalaupapa to the west and Kalawao to the east, Kalaupapa was the more suitable for human habitation. It was not until 1873, however, that the government paved the way for settlement at Kalaupapa by annexing a portion of the area to ease the overcrowded conditions at Kalawao. This joint but segregated existence would endure until 1895, at which time the Board of Health coerced the remainder of the original inhabitants to vacate the lands, with offers of money as well as land exchanges. When that failed, printed eviction notices were nailed to trees near their huts.

Although there were a few in the beginning who came to Kalawao and tried briefly, no one would stay or have much effect on the terrible conditions in which those afflicted were forced to live. Only after the colony had been in existence for seven tragic years would a change begin. It would come like a new whisper in the wind, a whisper that was faint in the beginning, but one that steadily grew in intensity until it reached that of a mighty gale as it roared across the land, sweeping away with it all of the old that stood in its path.

The Port of Honolulu, as it appeared in 1857, shows the four modes of water transportation in use at the time: longboat, outrigger canoe, three-masted sailing ships and crude inter-island steamers. Hawaii State Archives

The spears that natives were using when the white man came to their lands ranged in length from 9 to eighteen feet and were made from hardwood trees. Preferred throughout the Sandwich Islands as the weapon for war, their tips and blades often had horizontal rows of barbs, enabling it to hold on to the target once it had struck. HAWAII STATE ARCHIVES

For ocean transportation before the tall ships and steamers, the natives used boats called outrigger canoes. Consisting of no more than a large tree trunk from which the insides were removed and a balancing bar added, their size ranged from a seating capacity for a few fishermen such as this one, to extremely large vessels capable of carrying many warriors into battle. HAWAII STATE ARCHIVES

An Islander next to his canoe. Wearing sun protection made from leaves, he holds the paddle which is used to propel his craft through the ocean's currents.
HAWAII STATE ARCHIVES

Lot Kamehameha, commonly known as King Kamehameha V, signed the "Act to Prevent the Spread of Leprosy" with the overwhelming approval of the general public. HAWAII STATE ARCHIVES

Because of the declining native population in the islands from diseases, plantation bosses turned to China to fill a desperate need for more laborers. Easily recognized by their straw hats, these Chinese immigrants cut stalks of sugar cane while being supervised by the luna, boss, who observes them from horseback.

HAWAII STATE ARCHIVES

A typical Sandwich Island family unit of the 1800s, including their pet dog and a bird house. Notice the taro, the native's main staple, planted in the man-made pond at the lower left of the picture. HAWAII STATE ARCHIVES

Intensely religious and devoted to his family, Koolau stands with his wife Piilani, their son Kaleimanu and a family friend. When both he and his son contracted leprosy, Koolau refused to be sent to Molokai without his wife. For 31/2 years the family eluded their would-be capturers by hiding deep in the forest. Never apprehended, Koolau was buried by Piilani in a secret place which she never revealed. HAWAII STATE ARCHIVES

Three of the many Provisional Government's soldiers who went in search of Koolau. The man on the left holds a Springfield trap-door single-shot rifle; the other two are armed with the newer type of repeating rifles that you "load on Sunday and shoot all week." HAWAII STATE ARCHIVES

Members of Hawaii National Guard's Firing Squad, Company F. They stand beside the graves of their 3 comrades. Two were shot by Koolau when they tried to capture him; the other was killed when his own gun snagged a tree branch and went off accidentally. HAWAII STATE ARCHIVES

A Priest For Molokai

*J*oseph deVeuster was born on January 3, 1840, in the small village of Tremeloo, Belgium. He spent his earlier years working on his father's farm, and in 1859, entered service in the order of the Fathers of the Sacred Hearts Congregation within the Catholic Church. Joseph changed his name to Brother Damien as the rules of the order dictated and was put to work as a choir brother in the church. His superiors, realizing that Brother Damien had a strong, spiritual fire ablaze within him and was of exceptional quality and self-determination, soon allowed Damien to be placed among the novices studying for the priesthood.

Father Pamphile, Damien's older brother by three years, was also in the same order of the church and had been instrumental in bringing young Joseph to enter the congregation. When Damien was well advanced in his studies, there came the day when a number of priests, brothers and sisters of the Sacred Hearts were selected to journey to the Sandwich Islands as missionaries. Father Pamphile was one of those chosen. Shortly before the departure date, however, he became sick with typhus fever and was unable to make the sailing. Seizing the opportunity that fate seemed to have presented to him, Brother Damien asked to take Pamphile's place, and his request was granted.

After 148 weary days at sea, Brother Damien and the other missionaries arrived at the Port of Honolulu on Oahu. Damien spent two months at the Sacred Hearts Fathers Missions College in Ahuimanu, where he received the remainder of the schooling that led to his ordination. On May 21, 1864, at the historic Cathedral of Our Lady of Peace in Honolulu, Father Damien said his first Mass as a Catholic priest. Shortly afterward, accompanied by his superior Bishop Louis Maigret, he and another newly-ordained priest set sail for the Big Island of Hawaii, several hundred miles east. Damien would spend 8 years, many of them alone, working in two large mission districts on that island.

As he entered into his ninth year as a priest, Father Damien received an invitation from Bishop Maigret to attend the dedication of a new church, St. Anthony's, in Wailuku, Maui. While Damien was there, the subject of hundreds of leprosy victims who were exiled to the Kalaupapa Peninsula came to the attention of the general public in a newspaper article published on Oahu. On April 15, 1873, after an overview of what was happening at Kalawao, the paper, *Ka Nu Hou*, said: "If a noble Christian priest, preacher or sister would be inspired to go and sacrifice a life to console these poor wretches, that would be a royal soul to shine forever on a throne reared by human love."

A little more than 25% of those dropped off and abandoned at the peninsula were of the Catholic faith, and a priest was needed for them on a full-time basis instead of the occasional visits that were being made. Father Damien was the first to offer his services. Three other priests also stepped forward after him, and it was decided that they should rotate with one another. In this way, none of them would have to stay on an annual basis. Since Father Damien was the first to volunteer, he would be the first to serve on Molokai.

On May 10, 1873, Father Damien and his bishop landed on the Kalaupapa Peninsula. The only things the younger priest brought with him were his crucifix, his breviary and the clothes he wore on his back. Nothing in Damien's life could have prepared him for a scene of such human suffering that stood before his eyes. There were nearly 800 leprosy victims scattered over an area in which there was no resemblance of a civilized society. The average life span of those banished to Kalawao was about 4 years. Leprosy victims were arriving on the peninsula at a rate of about 14 a week, while their deaths amounted to about one third of that number in the same period of time. The number was staggering, considering that there were no stores, medical supplies or anyone in charge. In the Islands there was already a saying about Kalawao: "A ole kanawai ma keia wahi." "In this place there is no law." Indeed, for many who had been cast upon this land, there was none.

Amid all of these despicable shambles there were some structures that gave evidence that others in the past had tried to help at Kalawao. Behind a fence was a small group of empty buildings that had been built with the plan that one day they would be staffed with medical help. Two tiny chapels also stood several hundred yards from each other. On a small knoll was the Siloama Congregational Church, or The Church of the Healing Springs, completed on October 28,1871. Its name came from the Old Testament after the healing waters of a pool in Jerusalem. The other was a small Catholic chapel called St. Philomena, located east of the Siloama Church. The structure, built in 1872 by Brother Bertrand from Honolulu and a native helper, had taken six weeks to construct. The chapel's name came from a teen-aged Grecian martyr, who lived during the days of the Roman Empire. After having been hidden away for nearly 1700 years, her remains were discovered within the dusty Catholic catacombs of St. Priscilla in 1802.

For several weeks after his arrival, Damien slept beneath a hala, pandanus, tree which grew next to St. Philomena and cooked his food on a flat rock. Adjacent to where he slept, there was an unfenced and largely unmarked graveyard. The prevailing tradewinds brought to his sleeping tree the most overpowering smells imaginable. To make matters worse, the wild pigs came repeatedly to the area at night to root up and feed among the shallow graves.

Damien decided that he must remain to help these people at all cost. In a letter to his superiors, he told them it was his wish to be assigned to the peninsula on a permanent basis and not rotate with the other priests as planned. With this, Father Damien, missionary priest, rolled up his sleeves and set to work at a neck-breaking pace that would never slacken until death overtook him. On the Big Island he developed his skills as a leader and a man capable of creating and carrying out far-ranging plans. Among other things, he had become a very good carpenter, farmer and improviser. Now at Kalawao he added to his capabilities those of doctor, undertaker, grave digger and at times, constable.

Even after his long work day was over, Father Damien made sure that he was not forgotten by those in power in Honolulu. He spent countless hours writing by candlelight to those in charge of the settlement, begging them at times, challenging them in others, even demanding items which were needed at Kalawao. While not understanding why others did not possess his boundless energy and concern for those with leprosy and the deplorable conditions at Kalawao, he besieged those in authority with a never-ending barrage of letters that found their way to the desks of his superior, the Board of Health and, through indirect channels, to the news media.

Throughout Kalawao, the unmistakable sound of the hammer in Damien's right hand echoed over the rocky ground from dawn to dusk as he continued to improve the living conditions for those banished to this land. With the ongoing shipments of new arrivals on the peninsula, the colony rapidly began to outgrow its limits at Kalawao. In an effort to relieve this situation on the peninsula's eastern side, the Board of Health acquired a portion of usable land near the village of Kalaupapa. Near the calm bay that fronted the settlement, a landing for the steamer's longboats was blasted out of the rocky coastline, and it became the major place for disembarkment on the peninsula.

As his fear of contracting the dreaded disease faded into the farthest recesses of his mind, Damien was consumed with doing everything possible to relieve the pain and suffering of his people. Precautions that might have been taken during the first few months after his arrival at Kalawao were forgotten, as the young priest blended into their daily lives as if they were perfectly well. He never forbade anyone from entering his house, nor did he make any effort to avoid bodily contact with them during his daily work projects. As he had done when stationed on the Big Island, Damien sought not to hurt the feelings of those who offered him meals by dipping his fingers into the same bowls which their diseased hands had just fed from. Even when he paused for a moment to smoke a bowl of tobacco, Father Damien allowed his cherished pipe to find a place between the lips of anyone who asked for it.

Over the years, Damien built a number of churches on the island. Two of these located on Topside Molokai are standing at the time of this writing: Our Lady of Seven Sorrows was completed in 1874, and the tiny St. Joseph's Church, 3 miles west of Our Lady of Seven Sorrows, was finished in 1876. Because of his ever-growing congregation, he also found the need to double the size of St. Philomena twice and build a new church for the Kalaupapa Settlement.

In the later 1870s, an increasing number of children without parents or guardians were sent to Kalawao. These little ones were of the uppermost concern in Father Damien's heart. He felt a very special love for his children and made every possible effort to look out for their welfare. He treasured most those hours each day when he could spend time teaching and talking with the boys and girls. When Damien found a little extra time at day's end, he even made them toys from scrap lumber to play with. By 1879, after securing enough lumber from Honolulu, he began construction of a small dormitory for some of the youths next to his recently-built rectory.

On the Island of Oahu, Princess Liliuokalani of the Kingdom of Hawaii was aware of the work that Father Damien was doing at Kalawao. When a tour of the Islands was planned, she decided to spend a day with Damien. On September 15, 1881, clothed in a flowing, black dress, the princess was brought to the shore of the settlement. Liliuokalani broke down in tears at what she saw and was unable to give the speech that had been prepared for the occasion. Upon her return to Honolulu, so impressed was the princess with what Father Damien was doing that she sent him a letter with a striking enameled medal enclosed in a fine leather case. Along with the medal came the title: Knight Commander of the Royal Order of Kalakaua.

At the direction of the Board of Health, a German doctor, Arthur Mouritz, moved into the settlement in 1884 to provide full-time medical services. While this was some help to the sick, it did little to relieve the pressure from Damien's shoulders. There were still no nurses on the peninsula, and most of the ill preferred to be treated by Damien, whom they knew and trusted. When Dr. Mouritz moved to Kalawao, he noticed that Damien had a lively personality and was in the best physical and mental health. He was, however, taken aback by Damien's carelessness and indifference to segregating himself from the sick and dying. This included the traffic in and out of the priest's own house. Mouritz described Father Damien's residence as "Kalawao Family House and Lepers' Rest, free beds, free board for the needy..." which fitted exactly the current situation.

Not long after the doctor's arrival, Damien began to experience mounting difficulties in making his way up the steep cliffs that led to Topside Molokai. Slowed by increasing pain in his legs and feet, at first he attributed the symptoms to that of the natural aging process of his body. Some time later, however, when pausing at the end of his busy day, Damien also noticed that certain areas of his left leg had lost all sensitivity. He decided that it should be brought to Dr. Mouritz's attention. Father Damien sought out the physician who in turn referred him to Dr. Edward Arning, a specialist who had recently moved to the Islands. What followed was a complete physical examination, including the application of an electrically-charged platinum needle to the priest's arms and legs. The result of the examination rocked the very foundation of Joseph Damien deVeuster's life. He had contracted the same sickness that he had dedicated his life to relieve - leprosy.

It will never be known where or when the leprosy bacteria entered Father Damien's body, as the disease is very slow in developing external symptoms on the human body. There had been some spots which had appeared on him as early as 1876, but the majority did not appear until six months after Dr. Arning's examination. Perhaps Damien contracted the disease during the early years of Kalawao, or possibly at Kohala on the Big Island, when he often complained of getting an itching and burning

sensation when visiting the sick. No one will ever have the answer to this question, regardless of how much they theorize.

The Board of Health kept a large record book on the peninsula entitled, *Lepers Received at the Settlement, Molokai, 1879 to Present*. The only printing the large journal contained on its empty pages was at the very top and was divided by columns running down the full length of the page. The columns were titled: "Date-Name-Sex-Age-Nationality-Residence-Died." It was law that every diseased person on the peninsula be logged in the journal and all the columns completed except the last one, which was inked in at the time of death. Mid-way down on page 24, we find penned in flowing script and black ink: "March 30, 1886" in the first column, "Father Damien" in the second, "M" in the third, "45" in the fourth, "Belgium" in the fifth and "Kalawao, Molokai" in the sixth. It is an intriguing fact to mention at this point that while nothing seems out of the ordinary with the entry at first glance, in 1886 Father Damien would have been 46, not 45 as entered on the ledger.

Another noteworthy fact is that on most of the earlier pages of the journal, the word Hawaiian was written under the Nationality heading. Beginning in the mid-1880s, however, more and more names were registered as part-Hawaiian, a reflection of the racially diverse marriages. Also, a number of different nationalities began to appear on many of the pages as well. There were Germans, Spanish, English, Portuguese, French and even Americans who found their final resting place at Kalawao and Kalaupapa.

1886 was a year that brought great anguish and grief to Father Damien as the world became aware of his contracting leprosy. Yet, the same year brought him the comfort and happiness that comes with finding a friend to walk with him down the lonely path he trod.

It was during this year that Joseph Dutton arrived in the Hawaiian Islands and went to Kalawao.

Born Ira F. Dutton in Vermont on April 27, 1843, he joined the United States Union Army during the Civil War, and by the age of 20 was a lieutenant. Dutton married after the war, but the marriage failed and drove him to drink huge amounts of whiskey for over a decade. Throughout this lost period of his life, he worked at many different jobs and acquired a wide variety of skills and knowledge. One day, just as suddenly as he started to drink, he put a stop to it and spent the remainder of his life atoning for all of his past wrongdoings.

Dutton formally joined the Catholic Church and changed his first name to Joseph. Several years after, he heard of Father Damien's plight and booked passage from the United States bound for the Islands. Without announcement or fanfare, Dutton simply appeared on the Kalaupapa Peninsula and went to work with Father Damien. The two men were well matched in both temperament and mentality. Brother Joseph, more commonly referred to as Brother Dutton, was a quiet, soft-spoken and gentle man with a sense of humor. He was physically strong and proved to be a near equal to Father Damien at his hardest work.

Extremely patriotic, Dutton over the years at Kalawao, always had the American flag flying in his yard; he would allow no one except himself to raise or lower it every day. He was a passionate organizer and a spotless housekeeper. Without exception, he purified himself after handling the sick or the items they were in contact with. After his arrival, Brother Dutton assumed the role of nurse in dressing the sores of the sick, secretary, gardener, postmaster, housing manager and anything else which he was called upon to do.

While leprosy advanced within Father Damien's body, he continued to maintain his steady routine of comforting, planning and improvements as though he had never been stricken by the disease. By 1888, as a part of his body died a little more each day, it seemed to be replaced with someone or something that came along to fill the void he was leaving behind. This was a time that saw many changes as well as new faces on the peninsula, to help with the people of Kalawao and Kalaupapa.

In this year, the number of patients on the peninsula rose to over 1,000 for the first time and Rudolph Meyer, superintendent of the colony, inventoried the number of buildings in the two settlements at 374. In addition to those structures occupied by leprosy victims, doctors and helpers, there were 5 churches, two of which were Catholic, two Protestant and one Mormon. There were also 12 hospital buildings, one store, 2 warehouses and a jail with two cells.

Additionally, a wealthy businessman in Honolulu, Charles R. Bishop, gave a donation of enough money to begin construction on several "homes or houses...for women and girls" near the landing at Kalaupapa. Sent to manage them were Mother Marianne Cope, Sister Vincent McCormick and Sister Leopoldina Burns, who were previously assigned to the leprosy facility in Kakaako on Oahu since their arrival in the Islands in 1883.

There were also two new full-time Catholic priests that came: Father Louis Conrardy to help Damien manage his parish at Kalawao, and Father Wendelin Moellers for the settlement in Kalaupapa. The Board of Health hired an Irishman, James Sinnett, as a personal helper and nurse for the dying priest. Even with all his new-found help, Damien continued his work well beyond the point when he should have allowed some of the others to assume most of his duties. A visitor to Kalawao in 1888 described Damien as he built the second and last addition to St. Philomena: "You should have seen the wild activity he was directing, giving his orders now to the masons, now to the carpenters, now to the laborers, all lepers. You would have said he was a man in his element and perfectly healthy. This tells you that Father Damien seems not to want to stop until he falls."

As 1889 began, Damien's condition grew steadily worse. His arms and face broke out with numerous sores and the booming voice that once conveyed laughter and merriment became a low murmur. By February, his body was tormented by discomfort which never allowed him to get more than several hours of sleep each night. His temperature consistently remained above one hundred degrees, and he had to drink large amounts of quinine water to keep it in check.

Both the sick and healthy tried to talk Father Damien into relinquishing control of his priestly and other duties to those who were standing by his side. Firmly refusing to stop, no one could make him quit until he was ready to, or he became too sick for his body to continue.

As they sat in their pews, the congregation watched Father Damien say Mass well beyond the point where his crippled hands could grasp the sacraments or turn the pages of the Missal without great difficulty. Unable to pick up his feet from the chapel floor, Damien shuffled across the floor at a sluggish pace that took forever to get from one side of the sanctuary to the other. Mass after Mass he continued, even though it was no longer necessary or expected of him. All anyone could do was stand to the side while their hearts broke in pity.

In March, Damien's health took a decided turn for the worse. After saying Mass faithfully for all of his ordained life, Father Damien could no longer walk the short distance to St. Philomena to do so any more. Through intense efforts of friends, he finally was persuaded to move from his old, timber and straw bed to one that had a soft mattress, pillows and clean linen.

At the age of 49 on the morning of April 15, 1889, after sixteen years of seeing more hardship and suffering that any human being should be allowed, his eyes dimmed and a peaceful look settled over his diseased face. As he relaxed, his breathing ceased and life slipped away, leaving behind 1,150 other leprosy sufferers living on the lonely Kalaupapa Peninsula. As Damien wanted, this was the first day of Holy Week. Brother James Sinnett, who held him during the last few minutes of his life, said Father Damien went calmly and quietly and that he had never seen a more peaceful death in all his days.

Brother Damien in Paris, 1863. Shortly before he departed Europe for the Sandwich Islands, Damien attended a retreat with his fellow missionaries. While there, he had this picture taken and sent a number of small prints to his brother in Louvain to distribute among the friends he was leaving behind. He also sent a larger copy to his mother in Tremeloo. DAMIEN MUSEUM AND ARCHIVES

Tall ships fill Honolulu Harbor while others anchor offshore to wait their turn to off load supplies. After five months at sea, it was along this waterfront in the early morning of March 19, 1864, that a young and inexperienced Brother Damien stepped ashore and began life as a missionary.

HAWAII STATE ARCHIVES

The Cathedral of Our Lady of Peace in downtown Honolulu. Today, a plaque on its outer wall and a beautiful stained-glass window recognizes the fact that Father Damien's first Mass was celebrated here on May 21, 1864. After he was ordained, Damien wrote to his parents: "Now I am a priest, now I am a missionary in a corrupt, heretical and idolatrous country. How great are my obligations! May the apostolic zeal match them! In everything I do I must show extreme virtue, sound judgment and great prudence."

HAWAII STATE ARCHIVES

Bishop Louis Maigret, Superior of the Sacred Hearts Congregation in the Sandwich Islands, gave Father Damien his first taste of life as a missionary priest in 1864. As he had brought Damien to his beginning as a missionary, the Bishop also brought him to his end by accompanying the priest to Kalawao, Molokai, in 1873. HAWAII STATE ARCHIVES

Homes similar to this one were in use throughout the archipelago before and during Damien's time. Constructed of thatched grass and tree branches, they provided all the shelter that was required for the Islanders to live in the tropics. As additional rain protection for this roof, a tropical, broad-leafed monsterra has been planted over the top to serve as an umbrella. HAWAII STATE ARCHIVES

Father Damien's first full-sized church in the Sandwich Islands.
Following the method his congregation used with their homes, its walls
were made of thatched grass. This church was located at Kapaahu,
about three miles south of Kalapana on the Big Island of Hawaii.

DAMIEN MUSEUM AND ARCHIVES

As if the rugged land and elements were not enough
to contend with while working on the Big Island,
Damien sometimes had to struggle to keep some of
the people from returning to the many pagan beliefs
deeply ingrained from generations of practice. Here,
a silver-haired kahuna during the late 1800s takes
a rest next to his hut. Notice his left hand which
has seven fingers and one thumb.

HAWAII STATE ARCHIVES

After completing the impressive St. Anthony's Church in Wailuku,
Maui, Bishop Maigret invited a number of priests from other islands to
attend the dedication. It was at this time that Father Damien offered to
help at Kalawao with those banished to the peninsula.

HAWAII STATE ARCHIVES

In addition to Father Damien and Bishop Maigret, the inter-island steamer on which they traveled to Molokai in 1873 carried a cargo of humans: fifty men, women and children who were being exiled to the settlement of Kalawao. Typical of the small ships that made their trips to and from Molokai, this one carries a load of horses and cattle as well as people. HAWAII STATE ARCHIVES

33-year-old Father Damien the year he went to Maui for the dedication of St. Anthony's. When he left for Molokai on the inter-island steamer, it was to be the last time he would ever visit Maui's shores. HAWAII STATE ARCHIVES

In one of his many letters to the Board of Heath, Father Damien on December 6, 1877, wrote: "You are aware that for the general welfare of the lepers I have sacrificed my health and all I have in this world...Your most humble and obedient servant. J. Damien, Catholic Priest." HAWAII STATE ARCHIVES

By the mid-1870s Damien's efforts had brought about considerable changes in the settlement's appearance as shown here. Notice, however, the lack of vegetation in the entire area. Four years before Damien's arrival, a visitor to Kalawao did an inventory of the inhabitants' grass huts. His comments went something like this: "Hut number four contains...1 knife and 2 spoons. Inside is cold, filthy, wretched and it leaks. Its inmate Manaku owns 1 woolen shirt, 1 pair pants and 1 gray blanket. Hut number thirty-eight has 1 pint tin, 1 knife and 1 spoon. The woman inmate Kailokani owns 1 blanket and no clothes. This is the most wretched of them all..." HAWAII STATE ARCHIVES

The Meyer Family. Rudolph Meyer settled on Molokai in 1850 and married the eighteen-year-old High Chiefess Kalama Waha from Mapulehu, Molokai. Settling on land along the cliffs above Kalaupapa where they raised a large family, Rudolph was superinten-dent for the settlements on the peninsula for three decades. As a result, he and Father Damien became very good friends.

DAMIEN MUSEUM AND ARCHIVES

Getting livestock to the peninsula from steamers in the 1800s was not as simple as pushing them overboard. Often, the animals would swim toward the open sea and drown. As a safety precaution, a paniolo, Hawaiian cowboy, was stationed nearby, ready to herd the cattle to shore and safety. Livestock was also purchased from Meyer's Ranch in Kalae and driven single-file down the steep trail to the settlement, often with the loss of one or more when they stumbled and fell over the cliff.

HAWAII STATE ARCHIVES

Father Damien and the orphaned girls from the St. Philomena Church choir. Taken during the mid-1870s near the unstaffed hospital compound at Kalawao, it is believed to be the first photograph taken of the priest on the peninsula.

HAWAII STATE ARCHIVES

Princess Liliuokalani. Shortly after her visit to Kalawao, Princess Liliuokalani honored Damien with the Royal Order of Kalakaua. She wrote: "I wish to express my whole-hearted admiration for the heroic and selfless service you give to the most wretched people of this kingdom, and to offer public homage to that inexhaustible love and patience with which you strive to ease the bodily and spiritual sufferings of these unhappy fold who are deprived of the care and affection of their relatives and friends."

HAWAII STATE ARCHIVES

King David Kalakaua. It was while the king was in Europe that his sister, Princess Liliuokalani, acted in the official capacity of Regent of the Islands and visited Kalawao.

HAWAII STATE ARCHIVES

Father Damien standing in front of his yard and work shed. Behind him is the two-story rectory in which he lived and died. By this time St. Philomena Church had undergone its first expansion, the addition of the rear section that runs from the left to the right in the photograph. The original chapel built by Brother Bertrand is the portion on which the steeple rests; the hala tree Damien slept under can be seen at the building's right side. DAMIEN MUSEUM AND ARCHIVES

Over the years, the plight of the people on the peninsula came into sharper view in the eyes of the general public. As a result, many officials came to the settlements to see what could be done. Here, a visiting inspection party in 1884 makes its way from Kalawao to Kalaupapa. In the foreground is the Church of the Healing Springs, Siloama. Beyond is St. Philomena Church with its older, pointed steeple. HAWAII STATE ARCHIVES

The old wash house and livestock shelter of the 1880s located behind St. Philomena. Eventually, a number of animals arrived on the peninsula that eluded the chopping block and were put to good use providing a source of fresh milk. As they matured, these animals became breeders, and a sizable herd of cattle for both meat and milk became a reality. DAMIEN MUSEUM AND ARCHIVES

The Kalawao General Store supplied such items as rocking chairs, saddles, baskets, clothing and food items to the settlement's residents. The very nature of the store made it the center of activities and gossip.

The Kalawao hospital compound is shown on the road's left side and the settlement's store on the right. The village's stone water cistern is silhouetted on a knoll in the distant horizon.

Another inspection tour, this one during 1886. Notice that the Siloama Church has been rebuilt and now stands rotated 90° westward from the 1884 photograph.

A typical Corpus Christi procession, during which the people would march from Kalawao to Kalaupapa. Father Damien described one such event in 1886: "When all was ready, the procession was formed, the cross and the large banner being in advance. Then came the drums and the musical instruments of tin - may some charitable soul supply us with brass instruments! And then two associations bearing the Hawaiian flag, followed by two lines of Christian women, after these the men, then the singers - always directed by my good blind Petro, under a parasol and guided by another native." HAWAII STATE ARCHIVES

Mother Marianne Cope while serving at St. Joseph's Hospital in Syracuse, New York, in the 1870s. Born in Germany, she emigrated to the United States with her parents when she was two years old. In 1862 she joined the Sisters of the Third Order of St. Francis in Syracuse, New York, and came to the Islands with six other nuns in November, 1883. Mother Marianne worked at the leprosy facility in Kakaako, Oahu, for 5 years before arriving at Kalaupapa to head the Bishop Home for Girls. DAMIEN MUSEUM AND ARCHIVES

The Sisters of St. Francis, their young female patients and the President of the Board of Health, Walter M. Gibson. This photograph was taken in front of the Kapiolani Girl's Home, which was just adjacent to the walls of the Kakaako Hospital on Oahu. HAWAII STATE ARCHIVES

Patients wait in line for food distribution at the Kakaako Hospital. One of them has acquired a new invention called a wheelbarrow to ease the work of carrying supplies back to where he lives. DAMIEN MUSEUM AND ARCHIVES

A Japanese physician, Dr. Masanao Goto, visited Kakaako Hospital in 1886 and brought with him a new method for treating leprosy with different medicines combined with baths of hot water. Father Damien visited Honolulu to try these hot baths for a few days but left them unfinished, as he was unwilling to commit himself to any more time away from his people. After his return to Kalawao, one of Damien's well-recognized letters appeared on the desk of the Board of Health. The board soon discovered that this strange request was a list of ingredients that made up the solution known as the Goto Bath Treatment. Father Damien then proceeded to build his own bath house at Kalawao from discarded materials.

Hawaii State Archives

A deckhand's view as a couple of longboats are rowed from the steamer to the shores of Kalaupapa. "One could never imagine what a lonely, barren place it was. Not a tree nor a shrub in the whole settlement; only in the churchyard there were a few poor little trees that were so bent and yellow by the continued sweep of the burning wind it would make one sad to look at them." Mother Marianne. Hawaii State Archives

Father Wendelin Moellers of the Sacred Hearts Congregation, seated on the right, arrived to work at the Catholic church in Kalaupapa shortly after Mother Marianne and her sisters came to the settlement. Bishop Koeckmann, on the left, filled the position as Damien's superior after the passing of Bishop Maigret. DAMIEN MUSEUM AND ARCHIVES

Twenty-year-old Lt. Ira F. Dutton. All his life Dutton was a devoted patriot who dearly loved America. For a number of years after he moved to Kalawao he refused to claim the government pension check owed him for serving in the army, saying: "One would not be worth his salt to take money for serving the country which had done so much for him." At the start of World War I, although he was 50 years over the age of most soldiers, Brother Dutton offered his services and his old, blue uniform for duty on the front lines of battle as a sharpshooter. HAWAII STATE ARCHIVES

Father Louis Conrardy, missionary priest, worked in the Indian Territory of the northwestern United States for 15 years. As a result of corresponding with Father Damien over a number of years, he moved to Kalawao in 1888 to help the dying priest. He left the peninsula 6 years after the death of Damien and traveled to China, where he later died. At his request he was buried "...between the graves of two lepers."

DAMIEN MUSEUM AND ARCHIVES

In December, 1888, Father Damien was visited by Edward Clifford from England, an accomplished artist who wished to pay his respects to the dying priest. During his two weeks at Kalawao, Clifford sketched Damien several times. In one, as a gesture of kindness toward Father Damien, he drew the priest and omitted the disfigurement that leprosy had taken on his face.

DAMIEN MUSEUM AND ARCHIVES

In the second drawing of Damien, Clifford sketched what he thought the priest would have looked like as a younger man, twenty years in the past. When finished, he signed his name and dated it 1868.

HAWAII STATE ARCHIVES

On December 31, 1888, his last day at Kalawao, Clifford handed Damien his own thumb-worn bible and asked him to write something on its inside page. The priest wrote: "I was sick and ye visited me. J. Damien deVeuster." As he departed Kalawao, the artist sketched what he saw and included himself in the lower left, waving a white handkerchief over the crashing surf.

DAMIEN MUSEUM AND ARCHIVES

Photographed by William Brigham, this is one of the last pictures of Father Damien in the outside world. After his visit to the peninsula in 1889, Robert Louis Stevenson wrote what seemingly fits this assemblage: "They were strangers to each other, collected by common calamity, disfigured, mortally sick, banished without sin from home and friends."
DAMIEN MUSEUM AND ARCHIVES

Photographed by William Brigham, Father Damien's right arm is held in a sling made by Mother Marianne from a red silk scarf. "Look at my hands, all the wounds are healing and the crust is becoming black... I have seen so many lepers die, that I cannot be mistaken. Death is not far off. I have seen visions of the good God calling me to celebrate Easter with Him. May God be blessed for it." Father Damien, 1889.
HAWAII STATE ARCHIVES

Author and novelist Robert Louis Stevenson
HAWAII STATE ARCHIVES

Photographed in 1890 by Dr. Sidney Swift, St. Philomena Church and its tabernacle, decorated for Christmas Mass, appear much the same as they did during Father Damien's last days. In 1888, a number of Catholics led by Father Hudson, founder and editor of the Ave Maria Press at Notre Dame University, sent Damien two large tabernacles, one for his church in Kalawao, the other for the Kalaupapa church. In a letter of thanks, Damien wrote in 1888: "We had some difficulty in lifting the interior tabernacle on account of the heavy weight of the metal part...the canopy, though a little too high for our rather low church, comes right up at a few inches below the ceiling. It has a true monumental appearance..." He added: "Fortunately, although my hands are quite sore they are not yet crippled." DAMIEN MUSEUM AND ARCHIVES

The last picture of Father Damien alive was taken by Doctor Sidney Swift, who came to the priest's rectory shortly before his death with a box full of glass plates and a camera mounted on a tripod.

DAMIEN MUSEUM AND ARCHIVES

This funeral procession along the Kalawao road is believed to be the one held for Father Damien on April 16, 1889. Notice the still unfinished steeple over the new south-facing doors of St. Philomena Church.

DAMIEN MUSEUM AND ARCHIVES

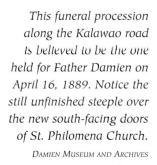

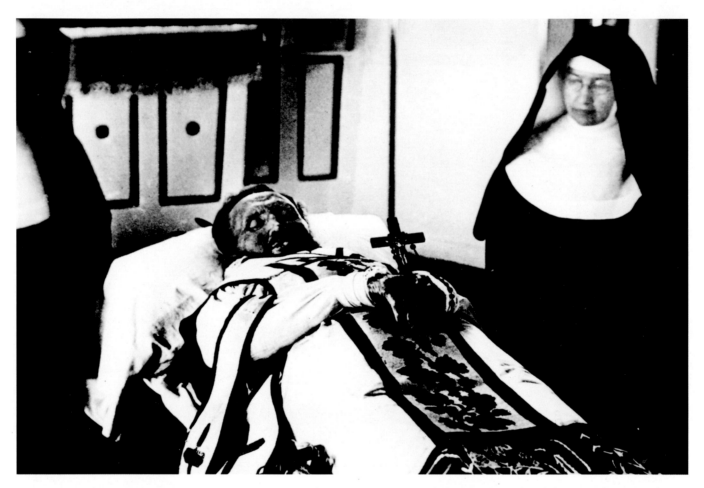

"I am gently going to my grave. It is the will of God and I thank Him very much for letting me die of the same disease and in the same way as my lepers. I am very satisfied and very happy." Father Damien, 1889. After his death, Fathers Conrardy and Moellers took the task of Damien's final dressing. Instead of his usual attire of black, they clothed him in his best white vestments. His body was then carried to St. Philomena and placed before the altar. This photograph by Dr. Swift shows Mother Marianne standing on the right. DAMIEN MUSEUM AND ARCHIVES

Life Without Father Damien

$\mathcal{F}$rom Mother Marianne's experience in leadership roles as an administrator, a qualified nurse and an educator, it was only natural that she was looked to for guidance immediately following Damien's death. The gentle nun was a kind and compassionate individual who never raised her voice, even if the occasion challenged her. Mother Marianne pursued life much the same as Damien in that she would tackle just about any job that came before her. Her figure seemed to appear everywhere on the peninsula as she became involved in jobs that ranged from digging holes for her trees, administrating to the needs of the afflicted, and washing soiled laundry.

Brother Dutton, by his very nature, was not the type of person who, when his roots were planted, took lightly to moving them again. After Damien's death, he saw to it that the priest's few personal effects were neatly packed into storage trunks and readied for shipment to Honolulu. It would not be until 1893, however, that he made the two-mile trip to Kalaupapa so that Father Damien's belongings could be placed on the inter-island steamer. Another three decades would pass after this before Dutton would again venture beyond the boundaries of Kalawao.

In 1892, Henry P. Baldwin, the son of a Protestant missionary on Maui, decided to provide help for the boys of Kalawao as Mr. Bishop had done for the girls at Kalaupapa. Construction was started on a complex of buildings across the road from St. Philomena; when it was completed, there were 29 separate units that were to be used by the boys and single men. Over the course of the next several years, the complex was expanded, increasing the total number of buildings to fifty. The Sisters of St. Francis at Kalaupapa provided Brother Dutton with helping hands for the boys until November, 1895. It was then that the Sacred Hearts superiors in Honolulu sent four of their brothers to the Baldwin Home to assist with the increasing number of youngsters.

Shortly after the turn of the century, the U. S. Congress appropriated over $100,000 for a combination laboratory and hospital to be located at Kalawao. It was the largest and most expensive project that had ever taken place in the Islands. It was, indeed, one of the best medical facilities in the entire world. Not only did it have houses for the physicians and their families, but for their 32 Chinese servants as well.

Built to conduct experiments with patients and perhaps find the cause and a cure for the disease, the U. S. Leprosy Investigation Station officially opened its doors for business during the Christmas season of 1909. Participation, however, was on a voluntary basis, and for this reason, the facility was doomed before it began. There were only 9 people that came to the laboratory to be tested during all of its days of operation. The station was a miserable failure which, for all concerned, needed to be swept under the carpet and forgotten. Its doors were closed on August 7, 1913; the gates remained locked, windows boarded up, and large Keep Out signs posted until 1929, when the complex was torn down. What materials were still usable were hauled off and incorporated into the construction at Kalaupapa.

By 1895, the last of the original settlers in the Kalaupapa district were forced from their land, to make more area available for those with Hansen's Disease. After this, unlimited expansion on the peninsula's western side became a reality. With Brother Dutton's death in 1931, it seemed as though a key was turned that allowed all of Kalawao to be shut down. The buildings of the Baldwin Home for Boys soon followed the fate that the U.S. Leprosy Investigation Station had taken. The home had served its purpose for almost 40 years. On December 24, 1932, the doors were closed, and the move was made to a new Baldwin Home next to the cliffs at Kalaupapa. When the operation ceased, it was like the final death blow to Kalawao, and the population began to dwindle at an ever-quickening pace. From 112 people living there, the numbers dropped to 61, to 28, and then plummeted to 7. Finally came the day when the last settler tossed an old burlap sack containing his belongings over his shoulder and without bothering to close the door of his shack, or even looking back, he set off down the dusty road toward Kalaupapa. With his leaving, deathly silence descended on Kalawao after decades of use. There was no longer a shipment day when supplies or people were brought or floated to shore; for that matter, no inter-island steamer even stopped on the eastern side of the peninsula. All was still now, as peace and solitude covered Kalawao like a blanket on a cold winter's night.

The Bishop Home. On the right is the Convent of St. Elizabeth, and on the left are the patient cottages. When the Kakaako Receiving Station closed on Oahu, much of its usable lumber was shipped to the settlement and put to use in building these homes. Robert Louis Stevenson, who visited Mother Marianne at Kalaupapa in 1889, wrote: "As for the girls in the Bishop Home, of the many beautiful things I have been privileged to see in life, they and what has been done for them, is not the least beautiful." DAMIEN MUSEUM AND ARCHIVES

Mother Marianne, Sister Vincent McCormick and Sister Leopoldina Burns stand on the porch of their convent with the young ladies of the Bishop Home. Mother Marianne, approaching her 25th year as a nun, and her two co-workers came to Kalaupapa on November 14, 1888, on a steamer with 42 patients, twenty-three of them girls.

Hawaii State Archives

Our Lady Health of the Sick Church at Kalaupapa was originally constructed by Father Damien in the early 1870s. While Father Wendelin Moellers was on the peninsula, his congregation was located here. Enlarged in 1881, the building remained in use until 1900, when it was replaced by the elaborate St. Francis Church.

Damien Museum and Archives

The Kalaupapa Settlement from the southern cliffs. Much of the arable land was put to good use, growing a variety of produce for the village's consumption. The Bishop Home for Girls, the Catholic Church and boat landing are located to the left and beyond the photograph.

Hawaii State Archives

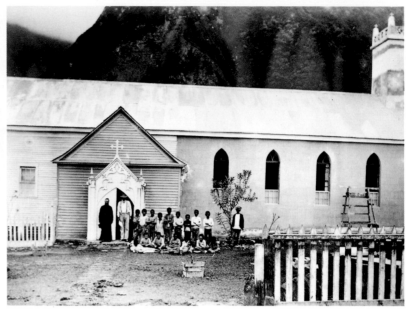

Brother Dutton visits the grave of his old friend and co-worker. DAMIEN MUSEUM AND ARCHIVES

Father Conrardy and orphans stand near the west doorway of the original chapel of St. Philomena. Father Damien's first addition to the church is immediately behind it and to the left. The second and final addition which Damien was working on at the time of his death is the smooth plastered area where the four arched windows are located. DAMIEN MUSEUM AND ARCHIVES

Visiting Father Damien's grave site next to St. Philomena is Bishop Gulstan Ropert on the left, Father Louis Conrardy in the center, and Father Wendelin Moellers on the far right. As a young missionary priest, Ropert was sent to help Father Damien on the Big Island during the 1860s. DAMIEN MUSEUM AND ARCHIVES

St. Philomena and the Baldwin Home for Boys. The home was formally opened in May, 1894, and its continued development and expansion was funded by Henry Baldwin until his death in the early 1900s. To provide increased shelter from the strong winds in the area, over 5,000 pine, ironwood and eucalyptus trees were shipped to Kalawao and planted around the buildings.

DAMIEN MUSEUM AND ARCHIVES

The Baldwin Home boys and their Sacred Hearts Brothers. The joint supervision of the home by Mother Marianne and Brother Dutton lasted until 1895, when four Sacred Hearts brothers were sent to assist them. The Laws Relating to Leprosy stated that "...the Baldwin Home is a retreat at all times open to leprous boys and men, who, through progress of the disease, or other cause, have become helpless or partly so. This home is not, however, to be used as a convenient retreat, free boarding or lodging house for those who wish to shirk all labor."

DAMIEN MUSEUM AND ARCHIVES

Standing on the west side of St. Philomena, the Baldwin Home Band show off their brass instruments which Father Damien always hoped some "charitable soul" would furnish. Notice the lone Caucasian boy holding the smaller of the two drums. *Hawaii State Archives*

Bishop Libert Boeynaems of Honolulu and six residents of the Baldwin Home visit the grave of Father Damien.

Damien Museum and Archives

Brother Dutton and a group of boys relax under a shady tree. As manager of the boy's home, Dutton subscribed to many periodicals and newspapers to keep informed with the events that were taking place in the world beyond Molokai. In so doing, he dutifully removed any items from the printed articles that might be immodest or unfit for the eyes of his people. *Damien Museum and Archives*

A group of Kalawao youngsters near Father Damien's rectory. At the time of this photograph, construction between the two buildings was underway to allow additional living quarters for the boys. *Hawaii State Archives*

When their chores were completed, Baldwin Home occupants frequently passed their idle time on the front porch. Notice the small boy, age about four, who is hardly taller than the benches on which the others sit.
HAWAII STATE ARCHIVES

Reverend Father Maxim Andre and Reverend Joseph Juliotte flank a Kalawao boy who shows the effects that leprosy has taken on him. DAMIEN MUSEUM AND ARCHIVES

Brother Dutton in his flag-draped office. He went to great efforts to remember special dates of those he corresponded with by keeping the people's names along with other bits of information in a bound brown address book. Dutton frequently enclosed small gifts from Molokai in his writings: a bit of sand, small seashells, photographs of himself and leaves or bark taken from the hala tree near Father Damien's grave. HAWAII STATE ARCHIVES

Brother Dutton and the committee from Washington, D. C., which was sent to select the site for the Leprosy Investigation Station during 1905. Among the officials and on Dutton's left, dressed in a white uniform, is United States Surgeon General Walter Wyman. HAWAII STATE ARCHIVES

Advanced in age, Dutton rests in a chair. Showing that he still possessed some of his original wit, he replied toward the end of his life: "It's a fine day, and I feel the sun. I regret nothing but I forget many things. I'm blind and deaf, and I guess I'm almost senseless. But I have no regrets." When he passed away, Dutton left behind few worldly possessions: his 128-page address book containing 4,000 names, a dried cutting from his mother's grave and 400 unanswered letters. DAMIEN MUSEUM AND ARCHIVES

The massive U. S. Leprosy Investigation Station under construction along the shores of Kalawao. In the foreground, a lone crypt keeps its silent vigil. DAMIEN MUSEUM AND ARCHIVES

Brother Dutton and residents of the Baldwin Home gather near the cliffs. Seated at Dutton's side are the four Sacred Hearts brothers sent to help him. The youngest member of this photograph appears to be a Caucasian. He is seated on the grass between the two men holding guitars. HAWAII STATE ARCHIVES

During the mid-1890s, Kalaupapa was well on its way as the leading settlement on the peninsula. The Siloama Hou, Hale Aloha Church, center left, was built to provide those living there a closer place to worship than Kalawao's Siloama Church. Hawaii State Archives

The Baldwin Home, pictured in the lower left, by this time is surrounded by fully-grown trees. The Leprosy Investigation Station next to the shore can be identified by the lack of trees and its white-trimmed roofs. Damien Museum and Archives

Our Lady Health of the Sick Church at Kalaupapa was replaced in 1900 with this much larger church, dedicated to St. Francis of Assisi. In 1906, a small ember of charcoal dropped on the floor by an altar boy started a fire that burned this elaborate structure to the ground within half an hour. Damien Museum and Archives

The Sisters of St. Francis. Mother Marianne, in the middle, is flanked by Sisters Crescentia Eilers, Leopoldina Burns, Elizabeth Gomes and Vincentia McCormick. Mother Marianne was a major force in shaping the advancement of the colony on the western side for 29 years. After a lingering illness, she died on August 9, 1918, and was buried at Kalaupapa only a few paces from the red granite cross that was donated by the people of England to honor Father Damien. Damien Museum and Archives

When the final move from the peninsula's eastern side to Kalaupapa took place, the old Kalawao store was no longer needed. Abandoned and empty, it was left for the elements and nature to claim. Damien Museum and Archives

A cattle-pulled wagon passes Kalaupapa's new St. Francis Church. Built in 1908 of stone to replace the brightly-painted structure that burned down, it looks today much the same as when this photograph was taken. DAMIEN MUSEUM AND ARCHIVES

Dressed in Sunday apparel, a Kalaupapa family poses in front of their home. DAMIEN MUSEUM AND ARCHIVES

In the 1800s, horses provided the major link between the different districts on the peninsula. In this photograph, a dashing young patient is ready to set off for a ride. His saddle shows the influence of the Spanish cowboys who came to the Islands in 1832 to teach the Hawaiians how to ride their newly acquired mounts. DAMIEN MUSEUM AND ARCHIVES

Settlement boys spend a day under a waterfall. The lack of water at Kalaupapa and Kalawao was always a serious problem for the people of the peninsula. Father Damien was instrumental in installing a water system for both of the settlements. Each was supplied by a natural pool and fed by heavy rains in the valleys to the south.

<small>DAMIEN MUSEUM AND ARCHIVES</small>

The Kalaupapa store with a few of its customers shortly after 1894. Notice the wooden barrel on the right, used to catch rain water from the building's roof. <small>HAWAII STATE ARCHIVES</small>

When supplies arrived at Kalaupapa during the early 1900s, they were taken from the steamers to the settlement's warehouse by dual wagon setups like this. The newer Kalaupapa store is located in the rear section of the building where the men are standing. DAMIEN MUSEUM AND ARCHIVES

A Kalaupapa police officer and his wife on the porch of their single-wall home. DAMIEN MUSEUM AND ARCHIVES

It was believed by some that riding horses was a healthy activity for those with Hansen's Disease. As a result, the peninsula even had its own race track at one time. This photograph from the 1890s shows a man and his lady taking a morning ride along the Kalawao road. HAWAII STATE ARCHIVES

Youth from the new Baldwin Home in Kalaupapa. Like all Islanders who love music, these two boys no doubt spent countless hours strumming on Spanish guitars. Their hats were woven from the leaves of the hala tree and crowned with the traditional flower lei of the South Pacific.

DAMIEN MUSEUM AND ARCHIVES

The members of the band practice as a shy, little girl watches the camera. In 1905, Dr. W. C. Wile of Connecticut donated $250 to build the Tarry Wile Bandstand for the people of Kalaupapa. The assistant physician's house is located behind the structure. HAWAII STATE ARCHIVES

Standing attired in his finest outfit, this Kalaupapa patient gives the seat to his trusted and faithful little friend.
DAMIEN MUSEUM AND ARCHIVES

John D. McVeigh, superintendent of Kalaupapa, during the early 1900s. Called the luna nui, big boss, McVeigh sits astride his favorite horse near his office, which was located where the staff quarters are today. DAMIEN MUSEUM AND ARCHIVES

The old ways join with the days of Henry Ford's Model T, as a group of Kalaupapa residents set off for a day of adventure on the Kalaupapa Peninsula. HAWAII STATE ARCHIVES

A group of young students gather on the steps of their Kalaupapa school room. The teenage girl at the top rings the institution's bell while another on the right holds their class' pet cat. HAWAII STATE ARCHIVES

Some of the boys of Makanalua enjoy themselves at a tidal pool. Afterward, they dry off on one of the typical lava rock outcroppings that surround the northern edge of the peninsula.

DAMIEN MUSEUM AND ARCHIVES

As Kalaupapa grew, so naturally did the rules that governed it. These police officers saw to it that law and order was maintained in the settlement during the early 1900s.

DAMIEN MUSEUM AND ARCHIVES

The steamer Iwalani was a regular visitor to the waters around the Kalaupapa Peninsula. In this photograph the ship's crew was making preparations to row one of the long boats toward the shoreline. DAMIEN MUSEUM AND ARCHIVES

For a number of years, patient David Kupele made the daily journey by horse up the trail to Topside Molokai and brought back the settlement's mail. When David passed away at the age of 86, he was buried in the lands he considered home, Kalaupapa. DAMIEN MUSEUM AND ARCHIVES

Superintendent John McVeigh and his assistants stand in front of the Kalaupapa Settlement's administration office during the early 1900s. DAMIEN MUSEUM AND ARCHIVES

The Longhouse was the place where patients and visitors were allowed to visit each other but were kept separated by a heavy wire fence that ran down the middle of the building from floor to ceiling. The Laws Relating to Leprosy stated: "The superintendent...at Molokai is hereby directed to have set apart a parcel of land...near the landing at Kalaupapa, the same to be enclosed with a double fence...so that persons may reach said enclosure and remain therein without being able to come in personal contact with any inmate. This enclosure shall be known as the visitors' compound, and no leper shall be allowed within it." DAMIEN MUSEUM AND ARCHIVES

Shipment day on the Kalaupapa Peninsula was always a major event. No exception was this one in the 1900s. The lingering question about this photograph is: what was going through the mind of the lonely, young girl as she held her hands to her forehead? DAMIEN MUSEUM AND ARCHIVES

AT REST AMONG THE BLESSED

*I*n 1935, King Leopold III of Belgium wrote a formal letter of state to President Franklin D. Roosevelt, requesting that the remains of Father Damien be returned to his homeland. On the morning of January 26, 1936, as the bishop, dignitaries and patients of Kalaupapa stood solemnly by, the spade and shovel cracked the earth's hard surface on the eastern side of St. Philomena. Father Damien's casket was removed from its resting place and flown to Honolulu. From there it went to San Francisco by ship and later was transferred to another vessel for the two-month crossing back to Antwerp, Belgium.

At Antwerp, Father Damien's remains received a welcome befitting royalty. The casket was placed on a hearse and processed through the streets, which were lined with an estimated crowd of one million people. From there it traveled through Damien's home town of Tremeloo and then on to Louvain. Winding through the streets, the caravan came to a stop in front of the Church of St. Joseph. It was at this church that a young Joseph deVeuster entered religious service and set out on the path to martyrdom, only to return to it in death 73 years later. After a Mass and viewing in the chapel, the casket was carried downstairs into a dimly-lit chamber, where final services were completed by a small group of Sacred Hearts priests. The coffin was then lowered to rest in a newly-constructed marble crypt. Its top slab was sealed shut, and it was decreed a national shrine.

The road leading to sainthood within the Catholic Church is a long and tedious one. It is filled with many obstacles and requires volumes of research that must be inspected concerning the candidate. On July 7, 1977, Pope Paul VI declared Father Damien "venerable", which formally opens the gate for further research by the church regarding someone's past life and is the first of three steps that lead to sainthood. The second step is beatification. To achieve this, there must be documented proof that a miracle attributed to the candidate has taken place. In 1991, the Vatican Congregation for the Cause of Saints determined that a miracle indeed took place in 1895 which could be attributed to the holiness of Father Damien. It concerned a Catholic nun in France, Sister Simplicia Hue. She was miraculously healed of a life-threatening illness that year, after spending many long hours praying to Father Damien to intervene with God for her cure.

The third and final step is canonization. To attain this and the declaration of sainthood, a second miracle must be evident and verified by the church. Those acquainted with the life and deeds of Father Damien feel that even though the official voice of the Catholic Church has not said so, the priest has already earned his sainthood. With only a matter of time before becoming official, sainthood would mean that Father Damien would be the first saint to emerge from the State of Hawaii and one of only four from the United States.

The announcement was made that Father Damien's beatification ceremony would be held on May 15, 1994, in Belgium. Meanwhile, Damien's crypt had been opened, where his remains had been sealed in ten zinc boxes.

One of these metal boxes, the contents of which are referred to as a relic, was to be given to the Sacred Hearts Congregation of Hawaii during the ceremony. They, in turn, would have the honor of reinterring the relic in Father Damien's original grave at Kalawao.

According to tradition dating back to the days when the Christians were persecuted for their religious beliefs, a relic, even though it may only be a small portion of someone's remains, contained great significance. Having it near is like having everything that the person stood for near as well. The ash and bone of Damien's right hand was the relic chosen to be returned to Molokai. This was the hand Father Damien used for the blessing and anointing of the dying, nursing the sick, sawing the wood and driving nails during his sixteen years on the peninsula.

For the relic's journey back to Hawaii, a koa traveling case, small enough to be carried by two people, was designed and built in Honolulu. Shortly before the beatification took place, the metal container was placed in the koa reliquary and locked. A seal was then placed over the lid's seam.

It was a great disappointment for all concerned when Pope John Paul II, who was to make the declaration of blessed for Damien, broke his leg several weeks before the ceremony. As a result, the beatification services were postponed until June 4, 1995, to be held outside the Koelkelberg Basilica in Brussels.

When the day arrived, the mood was joyous, although the skies were overcast and the day chilly. The Pope, positioned on a covered, outdoor stage adorned with ferns, white anthuriums and yellow roses, was surrounded by an assembly of cardinals and forty bishops. In addition, more than 500 other priests were in attendance. King Albert II of Belgium and Mother Teresa of India, long-time admirers and advocates for Damien's sainthood, were two of those in the audience. At the conclusion of the beatification, the holy relic was officially handed over to Randal Watanuki and Meli Pili, Kalaupapa residents, and to Very Reverend Joseph Bukoski III, Superior of the Sacred Hearts Fathers in Hawaii, for reinterment at the Kalaupapa Peninsula. At a special Mass the following day, Father Bukoski broke the seal on the reliquary and removed the zinc container. The relic was then carefully wrapped separately in two traditional Hawaiian kapa, cloth, which had been made especially for the occasion.

It was a memorable occasion when the holy relic returned to Hawaii. For seven weeks, the reliquary was taken to each of the inhabited islands, where it was the object of veneration and devotion by thousands of people. On the tiny Island of Molokai, everyone patiently waited as it traveled from island to island and town to town, giving the people a chance to pay their respects. The people of Molokai anxiously awaited the relic's arrival, and they were content with the understanding that their turn would come last. Once the relic of Father Damien reached their shores, it would never leave again.

On the morning of July 21, 1995, the relic of Blessed Damien arrived at Molokai's Hoolehua airport where it was met by a number of dignitaries. In a mile-long motorcade, it was then escorted to the three Catholic Churches located on Topside Molokai. At each, short services were followed by the opportunity for all present to go before the sealed koa reliquary to honor Father Damien. Later that afternoon, the relic was returned to the airport and flown to Kalaupapa, where a special Mass was said that evening.

The following day brought intense excitement to the little settlement of Kalaupapa. At first light, groups of people dotted the cliff as they descended the narrow trail to the peninsula; however, most visitors that day traveled to

Kalaupapa by plane. In all the years of its existence, the peninsula's airstrip had never seen so many aircraft in one day!

The entire Kalaupapa Peninsula buzzed with activity that morning. It had not been the subject of such a gathering of people and attention for many decades. The few rusty cars that belonged to the former patients and kokua, helpers, were kept busy during the early hours, shuttling people from Kalaupapa to Kalawao. The road from Kalaupapa was lined with hundreds of yellow ribbons, beckoning the way to the St. Philomena Church. At the long-vacated settlement, people from all walks of life gathered on the lawn where Father Damien's rectory had been. To the east by the old unmarked graveyard, an outdoor altar had been erected where, for several hours, services and Mass were held for the entire assembly. As the ceremonies began, the overcast skies that were present in the early morning disappeared, and the entire peninsula became covered by blue skies dotted with occasional billowy clouds.

After services were concluded, the people made their way down the dusty road back to Kalaupapa. In the true spirit of aloha, several hundred people gathered under the shade trees outside McVeigh Hall to attended a luau to honor the day which would be remembered always. Meanwhile, back in uninhabited Kalawao, the last of the living had departed, leaving behind only a quietness that can be understood from having visited that place. The only movement within the district came from the wild pigs that still dug and darted among the fields of grass-covered graves, and the winds which whispered softly to the branches of the ironwood and eucalyptus trees, telling them of distant travels to faraway places. Just as he watched over his flock as he lived, Father Damien was there now, to watch over them after death. Yes, the long journey was at an end for the farm boy turned missionary priest. Now, he could truly rest in peace where he belonged, at Kalawao and with the blessed. Aloha, E Kamiano! Welcome home, Father Damien!

Bishop Stephen Alencastre and officials watch as Father Damien's coffin is loaded on a hearse for its departure from the Kalaupapa Peninsula. In an effort to keep his remains at Kalawao, the residents of Kalaupapa forwarded a letter to government officials: "We ask with our whole hearts your sympathy and privilege to maintain the body of Father Damien...Do you separate a father from his son...?"

Damien Museum and Archives

Damien's remains were transported to Oahu in an army bomber with a squadron of military airplanes as escorts. The newly-opened Kalaupapa airstrip offered for the first time a bird's eye view of the settlement. To the left of the road that leads to the landing is St. Francis Catholic Church. On the far right is the Kanaana Hou Church.

DAMIEN MUSEUM AND ARCHIVES

After services at Our Lady of Peace Cathedral in Honolulu, the casket was placed on an open military vehicle and processed through the streets of Honolulu to the accompaniment of ringing cathedral bells. At Honolulu Harbor, the crowds bidding farewell stood many feet deep along the docks as Damien's remains were lifted aboard the ship Republic. Captain Edgar S. McLellan, skipper of the vessel, was on board when it departed Honolulu and was at the helm when the ship approached the California coast. He was nowhere to be found, however, when it docked in San Francisco. There is an old tale told by the people of Hawaii that is still believed by many: if the bones of an alii, chief, are taken from the shores of their land, those responsible for the departure shall have a terrible punishment inflicted upon them. To this day, it is still an unsolved mystery as to what became of McLellan. DAMIEN MUSEUM AND ARCHIVES

In California, the remains of Father Damien were placed on the Belgian sailing vessel Mercator for the voyage to Antwerp, Belgium. Once in Antwerp, Damien's funeral carriage, draped in white cloth and drawn by six magnificent white horses, made its way through the city's streets which were packed shoulder-to-shoulder with people. DAMIEN MUSEUM AND ARCHIVES

From the Cathedral of the Holy Virgin in Antwerp the procession continued by automobile through Damien's home town of Tremeloo and on to Louvain and the Church of St. Joseph. After Mass was completed, his remains were placed within this marble vault and the lid sealed. DAMIEN MUSEUM AND ARCHIVES

The beatification ceremonies for Father Damien in 1995 were conducted at the sixth largest church in the world, the Koelkelberg Basilica. The group that gathered to honor him that day was estimated at 25,000 people, with millions more watching on television.

HAWAII CATHOLIC HERALD & LISA BENOIT

The ceremonies included choirs singing, as fluttering banners and flaming torches were held high above the crowd. Coline Aiu, with the hula group Halau Hula O Maiki, set the rhythm with an Island drum, while a special dance created in honor of Father Damien was performed by barefoot dancers, soaking wet from the heavy downpour. One of them later commented: "My heart was so full as I danced before the Pope that the rain didn't matter. It was raining so hard I didn't know I was crying until I tasted the salt of my tears."
HAWAII CATHOLIC HERALD & LISA BENOIT

Along with Mother Teresa and other noted dignitaries, there were over 100 residents from Hawaii, including a number of former patients from Kalaupapa who made the long journey from the Islands. Their brightly-colored dresses, aloha shirts and flower lei made them most conspicuous as they mingled among the drab tones of white shirts, ties and business suits.
HAWAII CATHOLIC HERALD & LISA BENOIT

Pope John Paul II was presented with an eighty-foot-long scroll, inscribed with the prayers of thousands of people from the Islands, asking for Damien's intercession. As the Pope addressed the crowd in French, Flemish, English and Hawaiian, he proclaimed Father Damien Blessed and designated May 10, the day Damien first stepped ashore on the Kalaupapa Peninsula, as a feast day, when the priest would be honored every year. HAWAII CATHOLIC HERALD & LISA BENOIT

Puanani Van Dorpe, on the right, spent several months making the two kapa in which to wrap the relic of Blessed Damien. The first kapa which touched the relic's container was white. This represented the purity of the church. On its border was a design made with black ink depicting two hearts and a cross, which symbolized the Sacred Hearts Congregation. The second kapa, the outer covering, was jet black, very thick and water-resistant. Assisted here by Carol Ward Aki during a special Mass the day after the beatification, Puanani wraps the relic in the first kapa. After both were in place, she secured them with a tightly braided ti leaf lei. HAWAII CATHOLIC HERALD & LISA BENOIT

Under the care of Father Bukoski and members of the Hawaii delegation, Damien's relic was returned to the Hawaiian Islands after the ceremonies. Its first stop was the Cathedral of Our Lady of Peace in downtown Honolulu, where Father Damien had said his first Mass. Today the large church is dwarfed by numerous skyscrapers surrounding it.

A statue of Father Damien located at the Hawaii State Capitol in Honolulu. Designed by Marisol Escobar, a duplicate of this statue and another of King Kamehameha I were selected to represent the State of Hawaii at the Statuary Hall in Washington, D.C., when Hawaii was admitted to the Union as the 50th state.

From St. Joseph's, the procession continued several miles farther east to the Our Lady of Seven Sorrows Church. It was truly a beautiful day at this larger church, built by Father Damien in 1874.

Eleven miles to the east of Kaunakakai, Molokai's main settlement, the relic along with its escorts stopped at St. Joseph's Church, the tiny chapel Damien built in 1876. Glistening in the early morning sunlight with a fresh coat of paint, St. Joseph was quickly filled, and the crowd overflowed outside, next to the cemetery.

At Our Lady of Seven Sorrows, the reliquary was placed before the altar for another service, duplicating the one held at St. Joseph's.

A final service and viewing was conducted at St. Sophia's Church in Kaunakakai. Afterward, the reliquary was returned to the airport and placed aboard a special plane for the short flight to Kalaupapa, the same airfield Damien's remains departed from 59 years earlier.

The area below Father Damien's large black cross at Kalawao was ready for July 22, 1995. Within the walls of his original grave, a concrete vault had been built, and the outside lined with freshly-cut ti leaves. Measuring 3 x 3 x 2 feet, it was finished in the purest of white and was waiting for what had been missing for so many years.

By nine o'clock that morning, the yard behind St. Philomena was overflowing with an estimated 700 privileged people. Those gathered on the grassy lawn spent a half an hour or so in leisurely conversation, while the Sacred Hearts priests in the church were removing the relic from its traveling case.

To replace the koa traveling case, there was now a different one, carved from the Island's hardwood milo tree. Located inside were the official declarations sent from Rome, the pen to be used for finalizing the documents and an airtight metal cylinder in which the papers were to be placed. Within this box the kapa-wrapped relic and cylinder would later be sealed and reinterred in Damien's vault.

The relic was placed in the sanctuary of the church, and each person present for the reinterment was given time before it. Some prayed silently with tears in their eyes, while others reverently touched the black cloth or slid their fingers gently over it, afraid that it might be bruised if not handled with the softest touch. As an unknown Island girl bows in prayer, clearly visible are both the white and black kapa which were used as a protective covering for the relic.

After everyone had taken their moment before the relic, they left through the door of the original chapel and waited for it to be brought from the church. When all was ready, chanter Marianist Brother Franklin Pao exited St. Philomena leading the procession down a roped corridor, where an outdoor Mass was conducted.

Happily married Kalaupapa residents Paul and Winnie accepted the honor of carrying the milo reliquary from the church to a platform before the outdoor altar.

With the assistance of his friend Richard Marks of Kalaupapa on the right, Kenso Seki, the settlement's oldest resident, is escorted to the area where the ceremonies were to be held. Born in 1910, Kenso was sent to the peninsula on August 23, 1928, and has spent his entire life there. He is the only living resident of Kalaupapa who made his home at the original Baldwin Home at Kalawao and was present when Father Damien's remains were exhumed in 1936. Still maintaining his sense of humor when told recently he was starting to look old, the former altar boy replied: "Hey, I looked this old when they took Father Damien back to Belgium."

Near the end of the procession, The Very Reverend Joseph Bukoski III, Superior of the Sacred Hearts Fathers in Hawaii, brought Father Damien's relic into the fresh air of Kalawao.

After Mass was celebrated, Deacon James R. Gonsalves, Bishop Francis X. DiLorenzo, Deacon James L. Carroll, Piet Hoedamaker, Sister Regina Mary Jenkins and Father Bukoski signed the documents, recording and authenticating the return and reinterment of the Damien relic. Below the platform and standing to the side of the relic from left to right are former Kalaupapa patients, Bernard Punikaia, Nelly McCarthy, Kenso Seki and Richard Marks.

Throughout the morning, fifty members of the Damien and St. John Vianney choirs sang hymns in both Hawaiian and English. There also was a beautiful hymn written for the occasion by Patrick Downes of Honolulu, entitled "Damien the Blessed." Father Bukoski, speaking to those in attendance, compared the surroundings of Kalawao to a natural basilica with "the heaven its roof, the pali, cliffs, its walls." He encouraged all those gathered to join with the choir and sing in their very strongest voice.

There were 3 copies signed that verified the relic's origin. The first copy was to be sent to the Vatican in Rome, the second to the Sacred Hearts Archives, and the third would be reinterred with the relic. Father Bukoski showed one of the signed documents to the attentive crowd to witness before it was sealed forever in the cylinder. Placing it along with the kapa-wrapped relic inside the milo box, Father Bukoski then positioned a lid on top and firmly secured each of the four corners to the box.

The honor of pounding the last "nail" was given to Nelly McCarthy, Bernard Punikaia, Kenso Seki and Richard Marks. Each drove milo dowels into the lid with a large, wooden mallet, covering the screws. Resident Richard Marks, shown here, taps one of the 4 dowels into the lid while Kenso awaits his turn.

With joyous hearts and voices that reverberated against the back walls of the natural basilica, the crowd joined the choir in singing as they walked the twenty yards from the altar to Damien's grave.

After passing the grave of Brother Dutton, the procession arrived where the relic was to be reinterred. There, the people were greeted with a floral arrangement that spoke from the hearts of everyone present.

After several prayers and many words of aloha, the milo reliquary was lowered into the vault and sealed shut, making it impervious to entry. In unspoken consent, those present removed their flower lei and, together with those holding bouquets, placed them over Damien's resting place and on the large, black cross above it. As each said his own prayers to the memory of Father Damien, the entire assembly joined together and raised their voices to sing Aloha Oe.

Franciscan Sister Davilyn Ah Chick strives to reach the top of Father Damien's cross in order to drape her lei of flowers around it.

In silence and with a final glance, those who had filled Kalawao with life that morning retraced their earlier steps back down the yellow-ribboned road. As they did, Father Damien's grave and cross were left covered with tropical flowers of every imaginable color and variety. "I am a leper, blessed be God! But please, and it's the only thing I beg of you, let someone descend into my tomb once a month to hear my confession." Father Damien, 1886.

Modern Times on the Plains of Kalaupapa

With the relic of Father Damien reinterred at Kalawao, our story has brought us forward in time to take a look at the peninsula as the 20th Century is brought to a close and a new millennium begins. With the understanding of what has happened over these plains in the past, it is possible now for us to revisit the different areas long after the dust, pain and sorrow have settled to see what remains.

This chapter is divided geographically into each of the three districts which make up the peninsula's whole. Visitors to the Kalaupapa Peninsula will see a number of the sites that are to follow; however, many of them may not be approached, due to their remoteness and their restrictive nature. Furnished with descriptive information pertaining to each photo or actual quotes of significance, we will first explore the district of Kalawao and then move on to the Makanalua District. Lastly, in a visit to Kalaupapa, we will see first hand what remains within this tiny settlement.

THE DISTRICT OF KALAWAO

Clearly visible from the air, Damien Road cuts its path through the Kalawao District's thick growth of vegetation. Beyond the peninsula are the lonely northern cliffs of Molokai which Father Damien and Bishop Maigret passed after departing Maui in 1873. There were once many villages in these remote valleys, whose inhabitants built heiau, temples, along the high escarpments overlooking the coastline. Some were dedicated to the shark god Kauhuhu, and others to various gods of the land and sea. There was also a place called the stripping hill where, as was the custom at that time, the bones of their dead alii, chiefs, were stripped of flesh before their burial. The people who made their homes here often traveled the coast by outrigger canoe or by hanging on to a floating log that the currents carried westward. At times, they would venture to Kalaupapa, climb the steep trail to Topside and make their way on foot to Moomomi, some 10 miles away, to catch fish and to mine stone for their adzes.

The Damien Road, leading from Kalaupapa to Kalawao. "The poor little cart and old black horse were sent for us, and again Mother and I moved slowly over that lonely road...when we reached the home there was a dead silence everywhere, the poor boys were in little groups...like sheep without their shepherd." Sister Leopoldina, April 15, 1889.

Along Damien Road, midway between Kalaupapa and Kalawao, is this site of an ancient heiau, built long before written history in the Islands.

The chimney of Kalawao's bakery, built after Damien's death. "I live alone...As for my meals, I eat only two a day...In the morning, I eat rice, meat, coffee and rolls. In the evening, I eat what was left from morning plus a cup of tea that I have to warm over a lamp. See, I'm not starving, and in fact I live quite well. I have so much work to do that I'm hardly ever home. I have to sacrifice sleep to write you." Father Damien, 1882.

Off to the side of the passage to Kalawao is a birthing stone in an overgrowth of lantana bushes. In olden times in the archipelago, it was at such places that the women of the Sandwich Islands came to bear their sons and daughters.

Damien Road, basically the same as in the 1800s, is still the main link between the peninsula's east and west sides. "I usually go from one church to the other in a carriage. On Sunday, I usually celebrate two Masses. I preach four times, and give communion twice. I have my two little pharmacies and always my little bottles of medicine in my pocket on my house visits."
Father Damien, 1885.

Father Damien's water cistern. "In the summer of A. D. 1873, we received some water pipes, and all our able lepers were only too willing to help in laying them, and in building a small reservoir. Since then Kalawao has been well supplied with good water for drinking, bathing, and washing, and has been proved to be a better place for living than Kalaupapa."
Father Damien, 1886.

Approaching where the settlement of Kalawao once stood, the land to the north opens up to a beautiful vista of swaying palm trees and the seemingly endless Pacific Ocean.

A solitary stone crypt is believed to contain the remains of a man from the Island of Maui. Oral history tells that this man found his final resting place in this spot several decades before the first victims of Hansen's Disease were banished to Kalawao.

From the road, the grounds between Siloama Congregational Church and St. Philomena are separated by a rock barrier which follows the gradually descending terrain to the edge of the ocean's cliffs. Pictured beyond the wall is the land behind St. Philomena.

Siloama Congregational Church had its beginning six months after the first exiles came to Kalawao, when thirty-five of these people began to meet regularly for fellowship. The church itself was completed a year-and-a-half before Father Damien came to Kalawao. During a reconstruction period several decades ago, a hidden vault containing detailed and valuable records from 1866 until the mid-1920s was discovered.

The area behind Siloama Church is referred to as Turtle Cliff by some of the peninsula's residents. In these waters a large number of the protected and endangered green sea turtles can be found, eagerly feeding in the bountiful and sometimes turbulent ocean.

The eastern view from Turtle Cliff offers the visitor a panoramic look at the district's shoreline and the cliff-like embankments, the result of centuries of battering by the Pacific Ocean.

It has been unnecessary for former patients and visitors to use any segregated facility on the peninsula since 1969. This small building beside Siloama, however, has been left as a reminder of the laws and regulations of the past.

Almost hidden by a large rock wall built over its center, half of this tomb is on the inside of the Kalawao graveyard, and the other half is on the outside, next to the road.

An excellent perspective of site locations in Kalawao. St. Philomena is the white building, while the Siloama Church sits hidden in the stand of trees behind it. Father Damien's cemetery is enclosed by a square rock wall just below his church. The smaller, diamond-shaped enclosure is an ancient fishing shrine built hundreds of years ago. The Baldwin Home for Boys was built just to the left of St. Philomena. Near the bend in the dirt road is where the Leprosy Investigation Station was located. The Damien Road dead-ends half-a-mile away at Judd Park, the eastern edge of the peninsula.

St. Philomena, photographed from where Damien's rectory was once located. Brother Bertrand's small chapel is identified by its wood-slatted walls, gray roof and the cross above the door. The reinterment proceedings held for Blessed Damien in July, 1995, took place on the grass to the left and behind the main church.

The interior of the chapel built by Brother Bertrand in 1872. Still seen today are the holes chiseled through the floor by Father Damien so that his afflicted congregation could cough and spit during services. Beyond the white railing in the newer section of Damien's church is the small altar built with his own hands. "In tears I sow the good seed among my poor lepers. From morning to night, I am amidst heartbreaking physical and moral misery. Still, I try to appear always gay, so as to raise the courage of my patients. I represent death to them as the end of their ills... Many see their last hour come with resignation, and some with joy." Father Damien, 1874.

Both Father Damien's first and second enlargements of St. Philomena are shown here. Almost touching the ceiling is the tall tabernacle that was donated by Father Hudson the year before Damien's death. "Kindly remember me to all the fathers in Louvain...and all the family. I am still able, but not without some difficulty, to stand every day at the altar, where I do not forget any of you. Do you, in return, pray and get prayers for me, who is being gently drawn toward the grave? May God strengthen me, and give me the grace of perseverance and of a happy death. I try to make slowly my way of the cross and hope to be soon on top of my Golgotha."
Father Damien, 1889.

The eastern side of St. Philomena. Father Damien's grave site is surrounded by a black iron fence under the second arched window from the left. Brother Dutton is buried to the right of the coconut tree which seems to be bending from the powerful aura emitted from the church.

The grave of Ira F. Dutton. "I am an old, old relic...still on duty, and happy. Almost ashamed to say how jolly I am. Often I think, we don't know whether our Lord ever laughed; but mine is ready to burst out any moment."
Brother Dutton, 1930.

Today it is difficult to believe that this was once a place of such pain and hardship. The unmarked field beyond the low rock wall is where Father Damien buried so many of his people during the 1800s. "The cemetery, the church and presbytery form one enclosure. Thus at night time I am the sole keeper of this garden of the dead, where my spiritual children lie at rest. My greatest pleasure is to go there to say my beads, and meditate on that unending happiness which so many of them are already enjoying." Father Damien, 1880.

"The principal graveyard back of my cabin has but two thousand graves and nearly one thousand are buried elsewhere...Ten funerals last week, three today, and two are now being prepared for death. Yet the number increases from day to day..." Father Damien, 1887. Today, the old graveyard shows abundant evidence that even after 130 years, the wild pigs still come to these fields to root in the earth for their meals. A lone tobacco plant at the right is only a fragment of the many which now cover the peninsula. Unknown when or by whom planted, their lineage could even possibly be from those that Father Damien once smoked.

Wild pigs, descendants of those raised by the ancient settlers on the peninsula, can still be found roaming freely throughout the three districts today. Because the residents of Kalaupapa provide food for them in certain locations, a number of these animals will come running up to an automobile for a handout as soon as the sound of its approach is heard.

These two and one-half acres of land across from St. Philomena were once filled with the Baldwin Home for Boys complex. When the move to Kalaupapa was made in 1932, everything that could be used in the new settlement was carried off. All else was reclaimed by nature.

Only a few objects remain to bear testimony that the Baldwin Home was ever at this place: a huge fireplace and some pieces of stone that were too heavy to be moved.

St. Philomena Church under the walls of its "natural basilica." Numerous boulders still litter the ground in the same position where they landed after the peninsula's volcano first hurled them through the air half a million years ago.

A diamond-shaped fishing shrine built by the earliest settlers is located a short distance from the lava field east of St. Philomena Church. It is said to have been used by the Islanders for ceremonies in pursuit of a bountiful ocean catch and as a navigation marker for the fishermen in their canoes while at sea.

Like bleached bones from a mammoth whale, the concrete pilings from the U.S. Leprosy Investigation Station endure little change as the decades slowly pass in Kalawao.

The eastern end of Damien Road. The pointed island in the distance is called Okala, and the horizontal island is Mokapu. They are covered with a thick growth of fan palms which provided entertainment for the early Hawaiians. The young, native men who lived in nearby valleys would swim out to these islands and braid palm leaves into a parachute of sorts. Then, they would leap off the upper slopes and allow the strong tradewinds to carry them flying across the water toward Kalawao.

Judd Park is at the end of Damien Road. The park is used today by the few who take a short break during their tour of the peninsula or the friendly cats that come begging for a handout when someone stops by.

Rarely are the waters along the peninsula's edge as calm as this day. The coastline where the surf is breaking and Waikolu Valley just beyond are where the first exiles crawled ashore beginning in 1866, and were forced to make their way inland to Kalawao. In this place where man is now the intruder, only the many sea birds and fish travel along this flawless and pristine coast toward Cape Halawa.

Reversing course from Judd park, our gaze turns toward northern Kalawao and beyond, to the District of Makanalua. The more that the Kalaupapa Peninsula protrudes into the relentless winds, the more barren and desolate these lands become.

"We have often said that the poor outcast lepers of Molokai, without physician or pastor, afforded an opportunity for the exercise of a noble Christian heroism, and we are glad to say that the hero has been found. When the Kilauea touched at Kalawao last Saturday, Bishop Maigret and Father Damien, a Belgian priest, went ashore...Father Damien was left...among the lepers without a home or a change of clothing. We care not what this man's theology may be; he is surely a Christian hero." Ka Nu Hou, Honolulu. May, 1873.

These winding steps down a lava bluff were once used to carry supplies up to the Kalawao settlement. Small boats from the larger inter-island ships tied up alongside the outcropping while the cargo was hastily offloaded between sets of crashing waves.

Storms were, and still are, frequent along the Kalawao coast. Very little of what grew in this coastal zone could be used by those afflicted in the settlement. The ground was hard-crusted, and seldom was there sufficient rain to water any plants. It was a different matter, however, along the southern cliffs, where there is rainfall in excess of 25 feet a year in some areas. Melons, squash, taro and banana grew in great abundance in these valleys; the problem for the sick, however, was to complete the journey there and back.

Hand-placed and without the use of mortar, this Kalawao house foundation weathers both the elements of nature and passing of time.

The only activities this savage area has known is the hammering of surf and the denizens beneath its deep, blue waters. It was also impossible for those sent to Kalawao to harvest a catch from the sea, since they would have had to make their way over coastlines such as these.

THE DISTRICT OF MAKANALUA

The Makanalua District. Kauhako Crater is located at the peninsula's center, with its collapsed lava tube snaking northward. Damien Road runs from left to right, and Kahaloko Cemetery is the square clearing immediately below it. Holua Slide and the grave sites in the pictures to follow are situated next to the road leading to the crater's rim. Our journey through this district will take us along the outer edges of the peninsula from the photograph's right to the Kalaupapa lighthouse, pictured in the far upper left.

The aerial view of Makanalua District was taken from above these majestic cliffs, which have been carved into intricate troughs and ridges by countless years of rainfall.

The northern cliffs of Molokai have been sliced into broad, cavernous V-shaped valleys. As the waters sped down the rocky river beds, they carried along their path a flood of minerals. When these settled on the valley's floors, a rich, fertile soil was created, ideal for agriculture by the early inhabitants of the Sandwich Islands.

Waihanau Valley, between Kalaupapa and Kalawao. It was here that a 72 x 55-foot pool of cold water was located, capable of providing a permanent source of potable water. Father Damien requested, received and installed a pipeline from this water source to the settlement of Kalaupapa during the 1880s. Beyond the photograph to the left is the two-acre Kahaloko Cemetery.

The name Makanalua, given grave or pit, is said to have come from the fact that in ancient times, the brackish water of the 814-foot-deep lake at the bottom of the crater was used for burials. In the 1800s there were a number of native homes and cultivated fields for growing crops inside the crater's rim. At water's edge in the distance is the settlement of Kalaupapa.

A herd of axis deer graze along Kauhako Crater's slope. Originally from India, a group of these animals were presented to King Kamehameha V in the 1860s. They were released on Molokai, and under the king's protection, their numbers multiplied so dramatically that today, they can be found in abundance over the entire island.

Holua Slide, built long before the white man came to the Islands, is known as a place where native games of speed and skill were held. 750 feet long and 20 feet wide, it extends down the southern slope of Kauhako. Located at the top of the slide is a 70-foot platform of stones which was used as a stage to perform various ceremonies. On the northeastern slope of the crater there are two square structures, paved with flat lava stones. Each about 10 feet square and two feet high, they are divided by a wall through their middle. According to the old chants, this heiau on the northeastern slope is the most sacred of all those located on the northern side of Molokai.

Although the area near the summit of Kauhako Crater, Mount Puu Uao, is not classified as a graveyard, it is understandable why some would wish to have a final resting place with such a magnificent view. While there are not many of these graves, each one is as different as were the people entombed in them. Placed at the very top of Puu Uao is also a massive, white cross that can be seen all the way from Kalaupapa. It was erected in the mid-1900s for Easter sunrise services.

We set off toward the northern fringes of the peninsula with an unusual escort that paced in front of the author for an one-quarter mile. Almost to the point of being unafraid of human contact, the axis deer on the peninsula are carefully monitored to ensure overpopulation does not occur. Tall fences have been erected around the Kalaupapa Settlement to keep these animals from becoming too much of a nuisance. Even with these high barriers, many of them still find their way into the resident's yards.

As the distance from the rain-laden cliffs increases, the emerald greens of the valleys' tropical rain forests are left far behind. The land now becomes that of hard black lava as the peninsula thrusts northward toward its outer boundaries and into the continuous winds.

Ananaluawahine Cave on the peninsula's northeastern side is believed to have once been a lava tube that ran from the ocean to the distant Kauhako Crater. An ancient tale speaks of how some of the peninsula's residents took shelter in its passageway during a large battle. The invading force built a roaring fire over a portion of the cave, after which the men poured seawater on it, causing the top to collapse. The warriors then entered the cave by the newly-created hole and killed all who were within.

The entrance to Ananaluawahine Cave from the ocean. The story continues to say that before the slaughter, two old women had been stationed at the mouth of the cave to watch the ocean for approaching war canoes. It was their duty to warn their people should any of the opposing army be sighted nearing the peninsula by sea. They failed their assignment, however, because it seems the two ladies had been preoccupied at the time with picking lice from each other's heads.

In a never-ending cycle that began half a million years ago, the Pacific Ocean unleashes its fury on the rocks of Makanalua.

A maze of low, rock walls and enclosures almost cover the entire width of the peninsula. Left behind from days when history was passed from generation to generation by story-telling, it is believed that the walls were used as land divisions, property boundaries and crop shelters from the blowing winds. In the upper portion of the photograph can be seen a rock wall that divides the peninsula into east and west sections. It extends from the ocean almost to the high cliffs in the south.

This rock wall which extends from water's edge to the cliffs is the longest, uninterrupted man-made structure on Molokai. Where its construction was begun, there still can be found a large number of offerings: pieces of seashells and bits of coral lodged among the cracks of the lava rocks.

Referred to by the author as the Stairway to Broken Dreams, the size of these steps indicates that a large house once stood at this lonely place. Located at just about the most remote spot on the entire Kalaupapa Peninsula, why anyone would build their home so far away from other inhabited areas will just have to be left to speculation.

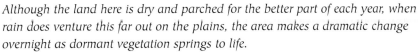

Although the land here is dry and parched for the better part of each year, when rain does venture this far out on the plains, the area makes a dramatic change overnight as dormant vegetation springs to life.

At every turn in this area, a labyrinth of squares and circles were built by those who once walked these lands. Without the convenience of nearby drinking water or shelter, it is impossible to imagine the thousands of man hours it took to collect these boulders, many weighing well over 100 pounds, and to build the vast amount of walls that run throughout the district. Some sites were constructed as heiau and fishing shrines, and others were built to hide the native's outrigger canoes from war parties from other islands as they passed the coast. Still more are believed to be burial platforms from several great battles which were fought on the peninsula during the 1700s.

Located at several places along the coast there are a series of openings where the volcano's hot lava did not completely join as it met with the ocean. Through these vents, called sea arches, there are continuous surges of water around the clock.

"This young priest, Damien by name, who has consecrated his life to the lepers, is the glory and boast of Hawaii...He is constantly in the midst of those suffering people, who live separated from the rest of human society as plague-stricken men whom the healthy dare not even approach, much less touch. He devotes himself entirely to their services; he dresses their wounds, and inspires them with confidence in their divine master and with the hope for a better life. Finally, when death arrives, he buries them with his own hands...."
The Commercial Advertiser,
Honolulu. September, 1881.

A Kalaupapa resident's weekend retreat. With only primitive beauty to offer, this cottage at the tip of the peninsula is remote enough for even the most avid get-away-from-the-crowd fan. Fishing floats, nets and driftwood from far-away places add a personal touch to its atmosphere.

As the peninsula reaches its northernmost point, the land is clear of the many volcanic boulders that abound nearer the opening of Kauhako Crater. Seldom traveled today except by archaeologists in search of a new find, this moisture-depraved and treeless land sits undisturbed in much the same manner as it did when the peninsula was first forged.

Next to a calm tidal pool, the pre-Christian settlers of the peninsula built this area to launch their canoes into the ocean and retrieve them afterward. By chipping out some of the lava's crust and replacing it with smooth, water-worn stones, they were able to slide their wooden boats up and down this ramp without damaging them.

Where the hard earth and sand meet, a fishing shrine was built for the people to leave their offerings. Still seen today are various shells and pieces of coral placed on the structure to make known to their gods the wishes for a bountiful catch and safety while on the open seas.

With a final look toward the east, our journey of the
Makanalua District draws to a close at Lae Hoolehua,
near the peninsula's northern tip, and the first sandy
beach along this entire coastline from distant Kalawao.

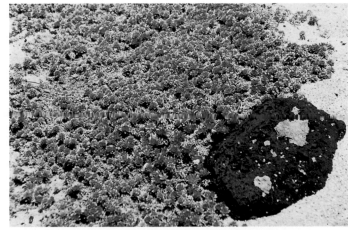

The light-green groundcover in the previous photograph is
the slow-growing Hinahina. Highly prized throughout the
Hawaiian Islands for lei making, the remoteness of
Makanalua ensures that it will not be over-collected as it
has been on other islands.

Even as far as the Kalaupapa
lighthouse and airport on the
peninsula's northwestern edge,
numerous land divisions and
rock enclosures similar to those
near Kalawao can be seen
dotting the landscape.

THE DISTRICT OF KALAUPAPA

*T*oday, the number of former patients who live at Kalaupapa are outnumbered by employees of the state and federal agencies who surround them. In low-toned conversations the question is frequently asked: What will happen to Kalaupapa when the last of the residents there who contracted Hansen Disease are gone? Neither the National Park Service or the State Department of Health knows the answer to this perplexing problem. The Kalaupapa Peninsula is the only national park in the United States whose land is not owned by the government. Funding from both federal and state sources provides the lease payments made to the Hawaiian Homes Commission for its continued use. It is unlikely, however, that any major change will take place until all of Kalaupapa's residents have passed away. When this occurs, it is conceivable that the maintenance expense will far exceed the funding that both agencies will be able to justify in order to keep some sort of development away from this consecrated ground. Let us hope that this day will never come.

For the present at Kalaupapa there exists a tidy little settlement that few others in the Islands can boast about. Gone is any resemblance of what the pioneers had to live in and around. There are a few narrow, one-lane roads bordered by closely-cut grass; nestled a few paces beyond are a sprinkling of well-kept houses. The residents' yards are filled with an abundance of exotic flowers and plants, tenderly cared for by their owners as they live peacefully and without worries. The cars on the peninsula travel at a top speed of five miles per hour. Because there is nowhere to go and no reason to hurry, it seems that the speed is maintained as if trying to squeeze the last bit of mileage out of the automobile before shipping another one in from Honolulu. Like Brother Dutton, these vehicles seem to go on and on, rusted and aged beyond their natural lifetime, but still going. The occupants, with their pet dogs sitting beside them, wave from the front seat, unconcerned about the gaping holes which once held doors. They navigate by looking through the windshield, if there is one, over where the hood, fenders and headlights should be, to see only the engine block, tires and an occasional mongoose as it goes skittering by.

These former patients may leave the Kalaupapa Settlement to live or visit anywhere in the world they choose; all prefer to remain exactly where they are, at home. The housing is free. All have food credit at the only general store, and they can have any sort of legal business they choose.

The settlement is a friendly place, where people's waves come easily and of course, everyone knows everything about everyone else's business. There are the administration building, post office, craft store, fire station, never-used jail and the hospital which, considering the size of the population, is one of the best staffed and equipped in Hawaii. In the center of the village stands the large town meeting hall, with a big blackboard nailed on the front and some chalk hanging nearby. Long gone and remembered with fading memories are the times when it was filled with standing-room-only crowds.

The only bar on the peninsula has a couple of bare-of-paint chairs and an old, wooden bench, where a few of the old-timers still congregate to talk about their youthful days, current events or perhaps to watch the University of Hawaii championship basketball game on TV. Those bare-of-paint chairs apparently became that way, not from the lack of paint, but from the customers that sit on them during the bar's short hours of operation drinking the two thousand cases of beer that are still barged into the peninsula every year.

The biggest event of the year at the settlement is still shipment day in July when the waters surrounding the peninsula are calm. The barge from Honolulu pulls alongside the Kalaupapa landing to offload, not patients anymore, but items that will be needed to keep the peninsula running for an entire year. With twelve months between supply shipments, just imagine what it takes to make a shopping list for the only general store. Offloaded are such items as hundreds of cases of Spam, a local favorite, and at this writing, 10,800 pounds of uncooked rice. Along with the food supplies are household and personal items too numerous to mention, and things like refrigerators, microwave ovens and perhaps a new Macintosh computer. Let's not forget to put in

an order for a few gallons of gasoline while we're at it!

A haunting and powerful feeling of reverence hovers in and around the many, old vacant buildings of Kalaupapa, almost as if they want to tell of the lives of those who lived within their walls and the dreams that were shared. Wildflowers and pili grass creep into the cracks of old stone crypts; the only movement found near the long rows of grave markers beside the roadside is the shadow of the sun as it slides silently across the peninsula. The darkness of night seems lost among the brilliance of a thousand sparkling stars, lighting the heavens more brightly than the evening windows of a large city. Seldom during the day can be heard any sound except that of a low-toned conversation, falling unheard beyond twenty feet, or the surf crashing on large lava boulders that cover the shore. The silence that comes with nightfall is even greater, interrupted only by the barks of many deer as they make their rounds through the residents' yards, sampling prized plants on their way. This is the Kalaupapa of the 21st Century.

For those who have the opportunity to witness a sunset on the Kalaupapa Peninsula, the colors offered by Mother Nature make a most remarkable and extraordinary beginning to the approach of darkness.

From the valleys east of the peninsula, the Islanders who once lived in villages along the coast traveled past these cliffs to Moomomi, 6 miles beyond this point. There, they would gather salt from the tidal pools, net the many types of fish that were not available near their villages and quarry stone for making their tools.

Today, the settlement of Kalaupapa is a closely-knit village of good friends and neighbors that requires only a 5 minute walk to get anywhere a person wishes to go. Notice the pristine beds of coral in the water which provide a haven to Hawaii's colorful fish.

With few places to pull off to the side of the trail that begins at Palaau State Park in Topside Molokai, this trail widens and ends at a stream bed near Awahua Bay, Kalaupapa, after descending 1,600 feet and 3 and one-eighth miles. Here, the visitor is now on the level grounds of Kalaupapa Peninsula.

Black Jack, whose home is high above in Kalae, gets a well-deserved rest while his rider is being given a guided tour of the settlement. After lunch, it's one more hour of work for the mule to make his way up the trail, where stables and green pastures await.

A sign at the bottom of the Kalaupapa Trail gives ample warning not to venture any further without an authorized guide. Another posted warning reads: "Hawaii law forbids entry without written permission. Violators subject to citation."

The sound of rolling surf can be heard as it meets with the Awahua Bay's powdery sand beach. In the shade of a false kamani tree growing near the high-water mark, those visitors that descended the trail to take the tour have their first close-up look at the deep, blue Pacific Ocean and breaking surf that surrounds the peninsula.

From Awahua Bay, it is a one-minute drive into the settlement. Ancient chants told that the best surf, most lobster holes and biggest turtles on all of Molokai were found around Kalaupapa, and it was favored greatly by the chiefs of the island. In 1867, a native said about the old days: "The waves are fearful, but the boys of Kalaupapa that were skilled surf riders enjoyed riding them. They are not mere things to be trifled with, either."

Although it was against the wishes of the residents of the Kalawao Baldwin Home for Boys, the home was eventually closed because it was too costly to repair the buildings that had seen almost four decades of use. A new complex with the same name was built just under the cliffs of Kalaupapa, because it was more convenient to have all the patients on the peninsula in one area. Today, one of the few reminders of this second home is its main entrance pilasters and a short, plastered wall.

Because of the availability of rocks below the cliffs, this gargantuan rock crusher was built next to its base and near the new Baldwin Home. It provided the needed gravel used in the settlement's construction period during the 1930s. Powered by electricity, it had a maximum output of crushing forty tons of boulders a day.

It must have been quite an occasion when the first automobile arrived on the peninsula. This old wooden-bed truck, left over from the days when there was still room underneath an automobile's hood, found its permanent parking zone in the brambles where Kalaupapa's Baldwin Home once stood.

Off to the side of the Baldwin Home's entrance is this rock garden built by Brother Materne Laschet. Referred to as The Grotto, it was intended to be a place where all who visited could spend quiet and reflecting times.

The old tack house, between the bottom of the trail and the Kalaupapa Settlement, was the place to store saddles and accessories when the era of horses blended with those of the first automobiles on the peninsula.

As our journey through the settlement begins, the unheeded words of a priest comes to mind: "I want to be unknown to the world, and now I find, in consequence of the few letters I have written, that I am being talked about on all sides, even in America." Father Damien, 1887.

The coastal zone at the settlement's southwestern edge is littered with thousands of lava boulders. Tumbled repeatedly over the years by the ocean, they have become exceedingly smooth from their constant grinding against one another. The white jetty in the distance is the Kalaupapa landing.

The Bayview Home for the Aged and Blind, which replaced the second and last Baldwin Home, was named for its commanding view of Awahua Bay. Located across a narrow lane from the bay and its rock-washed shore, it is the peninsula's third generation of housing that started with the Kalawao Baldwin Home. It is the first complex that was established for both men and women patients.

The roots of a long-dead tree cling to a chimney at Bayview. In a letter that was written 8 years before the first Baldwin Home at Kalawao was built: "I take the liberty to ask you to have the kindness of sending me one good stove for cooking sufficient for 35 to 40 boys, and also the necessary lumber for a dining room 24 feet by 16..." Father Damien, 1886.

Just across from Bayview, the cliffs of Topside Molokai begin their descent toward the Moomomi area, where the land is only slightly higher than the Pacific Ocean. Beyond that sandy region, there are another seven miles of harsh coastline before the channel that separates Molokai from Oahu is reached.

The settlement's small general hospital is overshadowed by the banyan tree that stands in front of its entrance. Maintained by the State of Hawaii, the hospital is staffed by nurses and visited by a doctor several times a week. It is strictly for the use of the former patients. The workers on the peninsula, except in an emergency, must fly to Topside Molokai if they require medical assistance.

The Kalaupapa Social Hall, with its chalkboard outside, originally had its beginning in 1915 and served as a gathering place in the settlement for decades. It also was used at one time as a 350-seat theater which showed movies twice a week. In 1958, the building was officially renamed the Paschoal Hall.

This Model T, belonging to Kalaupapa resident Kenso, operated until the 1990s. After it finally came to a halt, its owner shipped a newer and bigger vehicle to the settlement from Honolulu. While Kenso should have retired from driving, he is still out and about the settlement. Well-known for pointing his new vehicle in the direction he wants to go instead of looking through failing eyesight, most Kalaupapa drivers pull well off the road until he rolls by. The sign on his truck reads: "I fought Inflation - it won!"

The view from offshore Kalaupapa's landing gives a different perspective of the craggy coast. This area, where the Bayview Home, hospital and the Longhouse are located, is the southern limit of the settlement. The main part of the village is outside of the photograph to the left.

Over the decades there have been many religions represented by those who have called Kalawao and Kalaupapa home. This well-cared-for building was once a Buddhist temple that served the needs of the Japanese patients. Today, it is used as a mini-museum that displays artifacts from the earlier days on the peninsula.

Located in the middle of the settlement, Kanaana Hou Calvinist Church is the last of the four churches which saw their earlier beginnings with Siloama in Kalawao. The architecture used in its construction is typical of the style that was being used throughout the islands during the early 1900s.

Framed by the seed pods of a Royal Poinciana tree is the hub of authority within the settlement. Hale O Kamiana, the administration building, is where the branch office of the Department of Health is located and permanent records of former patients are kept.

Built in 1853 as a Calvinist church, this is the only structure existing from the 1800s that was built before the first patients arrived on the peninsula. The walls were erected from lava rock and the mortar to join them was made by melting coral taken from Kalaupapa's reef. Over the years it has seen use as a jail, repair shop and presently, a fire station.

The total number of cars traveling down these roads might average 2 or three a day. It is a matter of little consequence to the villagers when two automobiles meet along the settlement's one-lane roads. One driver just pulls off on the grass, the other stops in the middle of the road and they spend a little time talking with each other.

The only gas station on the entire peninsula, located across the road from the landing, was built in 1934. Constructed of reinforced concrete and measuring 12 by 16 feet, it has one gas pump, an air compressor, a lubricating oil tank and never a waiting line or a customer in a hurry.

When the state constructed a smaller and more modern facility at Kalaupapa, the previous hospital built in 1932 was set aside to one day become an exhibit hall and museum. It was a great loss for the settlement when the structure burned down, destroying many valuable, historical records which were kept in it.

"Mr. Meyer and I, we had today a look at the bad rocks in our harbor. I know a man living in Halawa who might do the blasting and I would say the Interior Department might assist the agent of the Board of Health to pay the necessary expenses. A few barrels of cement will be required too." Father Damien, 1870s. Construction on the present Kalaupapa landing and warehouse began in the early 1900s after raising the surrounding grade by four feet and adding a three-hundred-foot solid stone wall. In addition to supplies, the large storage building also shelters previous patient's records.

As long as they remain standing and in good condition, buildings at the settlement are forever recycled with new tenants after the old ones are gone. This one-time resident's home has gained a new lease on life as the headquarters for the U.S. National Park Service on the Kalaupapa Peninsula.

Bordered by coconut and plumeria trees, the steeple of the largest church on Molokai, Kalaupapa's St. Francis, reaches for the heavens. At the time of this writing, the building needs an estimated one million dollars for various repairs. Because of its declining congregation, however, the likelihood of receiving these much-needed funds is slim at best.

There are two sun dials on the Kalaupapa Peninsula. One is in Kalawao and the other, pictured here, is located in the yard of Kalaupapa's Staff Quarters. It is little wonder that there are not more in this remote land. Here, time has little meaning when counted by the hour. Its passage is best kept by the decades, if it is kept at all.

An anonymous donor gave this bronze statue of the Sacred
Heart of Jesus to the Catholic congregation at Kalaupapa.
Erected in the courtyard of St. Francis, Father Maxim Andre,
who replaced Father Wendelin, was later buried at the statue's
base. Although it is made of bronze, the statue is kept painted
white because of the salt in the surrounding air.

Very little is left where Mother Marianne once walked to
and from the boarding houses for the girls of the Bishop
Home. Only a field of green grass and an old stone oven,
whose opening is charred from the many fires it has
seen, remain. In the distance is the convent of the
Sisters of St. Francis.

The Kalaupapa Store is the
only place where those living
at the settlement can get
their needed staples for
everyday existence. The
blackboards on both sides of
the entrance keep customers
posted on what to expect
when shopping. The written
words this day seem to echo
a time from the peninsula's
past: "No meat this week."

As it has been on the harsh peninsula for ages, there always seems to be just enough nutrition provided by the land for man, beast and plant to survive. Across the road from the Kalaupapa Store, roots of the ironwood trees stubbornly cling to the small cracks in volcanic rock.

In 1891, Damien's friend, Edward Clifford, designed a red granite cross with the likeness of the priest cut into white marble. Raised near the boundary of St. Elizabeth's Convent, and close to Mother Marianne's grave site, it reads in both Hawaiian and English: "Greater love hath no man than this, that he lay down his life for his friends."

The recreation pavilion at the McVeigh Home. Constructed during the early 1930s, the complex provided individual living quarters rather than a dormitory for the patients. The luau which was held to celebrate Father Damien's reinterment in 1995 took place just outside this building.

A stone's throw from the Kalaupapa gas station is this open-air pavilion where a body can relax and allow one's mind to wander for a time. All of Molokai's North Shore is known for its profusion of rainbows; it is no exception here, where a person can have a seat at a rainbow's edge.

St. Elizabeth's Convent. There are three Franciscan sisters who reside here today. One of them, Sister Richard Marie, is referred to as the Fishing Nun because of her adventures to the rocky coasts with a bamboo pole to catch fish for those in the settlement who are too old to do so. In 1997, the Stick-Fish Queen, as she is also fondly called, celebrated her 60th year in her religious order and her 34th year on the peninsula.

Mother Marianne's grave at the western boundary of the convent grounds. By turning over volumes of research regarding her life to the Catholic Church's Historical Commission, the order of Franciscan sisters to which she belonged have begun a united effort which they hope will eventually lead to sainthood for her.

This Kalaupapa resident's weekend cottage stands at the northern edge of the Kalaupapa Settlement. The small house, with its backyard view that has unsurpassed tranquil beauty, also has what few others in life do: quiet neighbors all around.

The only bar on the Kalaupapa Peninsula is open from 2 p.m. until 7 p.m. There is not much fancy about Elaine's by world standards. Rest assured, however, the beer and soda are ice cold, the cable-installed television has great reception and there are lots of great conversations between good friends.

Nestled among exotic foliage are the Staff Quarters, commonly known today as Staff Row. The group of houses were originally provided for the settlement's superintendent and resident physicians. Today, the buildings are used by some of those who work at Kalaupapa on a year-round basis.

A short distance from Bayview Home, the water is so clear a person can see tropical fish as they dart about the rock-lined bottom. With a trained eye one can also occasionally see herds of wild goats scampering along the side of the steep cliffs.

Until the segregation ban was lifted, all mail leaving the peninsula had the corners of the envelope clipped off. It was then fumigated for eighteen hours in a special airtight container using formaldehyde and potassium permanganate. Today, the mail goes out just as it would from any other post office.

This resident's yard has a fence around it to keep the deer from grazing. Because of its isolation, the peninsula has never been a place to discard something that could be put to use. This is a good example. The fence was built from surplus wooden pallets that carried supplies from Honolulu to the Kalaupapa Store.

Under the direction of the settlement's superintendent during the 1940s, the dividing chain wall that separated visitors from patients in the Longhouse were removed. Today, the old benches in the building remain stacked on the table, while both residents and outsiders on the peninsula socialize freely.

Puaae Beach. From the Kalaupapa landing toward the airport, most of the land is unsettled except for a large graveyard and a few scattered houses. The beach front along this part of the coastline varies from a combination of sand and lava rocks to areas where there is only sand with bits of coral.

As her population decreases at an ever-quickening pace, more and more of Kalaupapa's buildings are boarded shut. Shortly after Father Damien's death, the number of patients at both settlements reached 1,166; soon after, it peaked at 1,200. As the leprosy epidemic began to burn itself out, so did the number of people shipped to the peninsula. By 1910, the two settlements held about 600 people; three decades later, the population dwindled to approximately 300 people. At the time of this writing it is only 56.

The bakery building. Since fresh bread is now flown into Kalaupapa, the structure has been turned into a craft shop, where merchandise made by residents and souvenirs pertaining to Kalaupapa are sold. The hours of operation are short, just long enough to allow those with a tour group to browse for a remembrance of their visit.

This open field near Staff Row was where the old Tarry Wile Bandstand was located in the early part of the 20th Century. Beyond the open area is Paschoal Hall, the old bakery, the jail and fire station, topped with a red roof. Hidden from view behind them is the center of the settlement: the churches, offices, housing and other associated buildings, including the landing.

Iliopii pictured here, like most of Kalaupapa's western coastline, consists of mostly lava flows and boulders. Because it does have the few places on the peninsula that are sheltered from the blasting of the Hawaiian tradewinds and ocean-waters, it also has all but one of Kalaupapa's sandy areas.

Ocean View Pavilion, north of the Kalaupapa Settlement, was built by the peninsula's chapter of the Lions Club. It is used as a place to enjoy fishing and barbecue get-togethers among friends.

As a beach front home waits silently for time to return it, like the owner, back to the earth, these words come to mind: "Almighty God intends to teach you not to attach yourselves to the things of this world. Let us remember that it is a place of exile, and that those who die in the Lord are far happier than you or I who are left here below." Father Damien, 1870s.

Papaloa Beach. Just inland from here is the Papaloa Cemetery. Referring to another time and cemetery at Kalawao: "I don't change much apart from my beard which is now turning gray. I am still living in the midst of seven to eight hundred lepers, and I have already filled the cemetery. If I can find another plot, I shall have...deeper graves dug and bury one coffin on top of another..." Father Damien, 1885.

Lying offshore in 30 feet of water, only the rusting engine block of the steamer Kaala is left after it ventured too close to Kalaupapa's northwest shore. Wrecked in 1932, many of her wooden beams and planking were put to use in buildings at the settlement after the mishap.

In a race against nature, the National Park Service is trying to save as many of the historically significant structures at the Kalaupapa Settlement as possible. First on their priority list, because of their susceptibility to decay, are the wooden structures, followed at a later time by the concrete and stone buildings.

The vacant houses around the settlement are found much the same as when their owners were still there. As a reminder from the past, on the dresser of this deserted home was a large number of colored buttons and 2 books entitled: The Teaching of Buddha and Techniques of Shorthand Writing, dated 1932.

Although they are expensive, casting nets for fishing in the surf along Kalaupapa's shores are left unchaperoned near the water's edge. Common trust among those who live in the settlement goes without saying and never will anything turn up missing on the peninsula.

From anywhere on Kalaupapa's coast there is an unrestricted view of Molokai's arid western North Shore and beyond. When darkness falls on the peninsula, a person standing at one of Kalaupapa's beaches can see the glittering lights along Oahu's shores, 50 miles away.

One of several neglected homes on the road to the airport. As people in the settlement pass on, the homes they leave behind can be occupied by another former patient if need be. This one, however, located far away from the tightly grouped settlement, found no takers.

Since children have not been allowed on the peninsula for decades, it is only natural that the residents have turned to share their love and affection with living things of a different nature. Dogs, cats and plants are most common, but for a select few who know where Ralph lives, there is a very special pet, a Hawaiian monk seal. Classified as an endangered species, Ralph faces the sunset to warm his underside during a nap. As this book went to press, it seems that there will have to be a new name found for Ralph: she had a baby!

The Kalaupapa lighthouse, with its 189-step staircase, began service in 1909 to protect passing ships from the jagged coastline during pitch-black nights. Originally, its 820,000 candlepower, three-ton lens could be seen from 21 miles at sea. The lens and the lighthouse keepers, however, were replaced in the mid-1900s by an automatic rotating beacon.

With Kalaupapa left behind, we head down the single-lane road toward the airport and our departure. If we had arrived by plane earlier that day to take our tour, the first major impact which we encountered on the way into the settlement was the Papaloa Cemetery. It is the largest concentration of cemeteries on the peninsula; all religious denominations in Kalaupapa have buried their dead in plots which adjoin each other's boundaries.

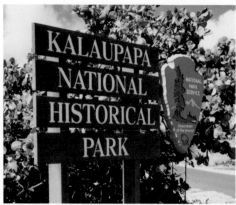

Next to the shoreline and within sight of the airport, the walls of an abandoned home bow to the powerful, salty winds that rake across the Kalaupapa Peninsula from lands faraway to the north and east.

Near the airstrip, a sign stationed along the road leading to the Kalaupapa Settlement gives notice that a visitor is now under the control and careful eye of United States Park Rangers.

The Kalaupapa airport terminal is a three-walled structure with its fourth side open and facing a pair of sea grape trees and the runway. Flights are twice daily, usually around 9 a.m. for incoming passengers and freight, and around 2 p.m. to return visitors to Molokai's main airport.

As we climb aboard our small airplane, we bid a final farewell to the lands of Father Damien and those who the priest had come to serve. Although the runway is short, it has ample room for today's aircraft to carry us back to a world of fast food restaurants and day-to-day problems. Often the rough ocean waves break over the airstrip's surrounding lava rocks with such intensity that their spray can be seen near window-level as the plane climbs skyward over the peninsula's edge and points its nose toward the west.

Stories Carved in Stone

*T*oday in the Kalaupapa Settlement, there are very few former patients left, and all of them are well into their golden years. As their numbers dwindle more with each passing year, the final sunset is rapidly approaching the land as it has existed for decades. After the last resident is gone and the old buildings have crumbled, only the stone grave markers and history will be left as a reminder for future generations as to what happened on these grounds.

The remains of those people on the peninsula marked with gravestones are the fortunate ones. There were no markers for thousands of others who lie on these lonely plains. If there had been, they were made from wood which by now has rotted and disintegrated. To take a step anywhere on the peninsula, it is possible that where the foot lands is also where someone is buried. These graves contain the remains of people of all ages, races and religions. For those that lie in these unmarked places, there are no names, no lifetimes, no past. Even though they each had hopes and dreams that would read like its own book, there is nothing that comes from the earth except silence. All now has been forever erased from memory by the passing of time.

Neither reader nor writer know who these men, women and children were that died a century or more ago, these sufferers who were cut down in the prime years of their life. They came from such places as Kalapana, Oopuloa Point, Kealakekua, Lahaina, and Iao Valley. When spoken, their names flowed over the tips of tongues as easily as does the cold waters over the stones in a hidden mountain stream: Pololena, Kepakiano, Amapolokio, Kekuanaoa, and Lokomaikai.

From the faded, yellow pages of the journal entitled *Lepers Received at the Settlement, Molokai, 1879 To Present,* we see that many were not even given the chance for their childhood to blossom with laughter or the games of happiness. There were the two little girls, Mileke and Kalike, both aged 6, who were sent to Kalawao on September 17, 1881, from different homes in Honolulu on Oahu. Mileke's short life ended on July 28, 1884, and Kalike's on October 27, 1886. The list seems endless as the ghostly roll call is read. Too numerous to be listed on the pages of this book were those who were six, seven, eight, nine, ten and eleven years old, although one day it should be called out for all to hear. Beka, age 4 from Makawao, Maui, was sent to Kalawao alone and without a friend; Kealoha, age 3 from Kona, Hawaii, was there also, as were three baby boys, Kaanaana, Kaalekaina and Kalani, each one year old. Although Kaanaana died when he was seven, the end of life for the two other boys was simply recorded as "no record of death." The parents and widowers of the people written on those pages lived on for another fifty years after their death, and even their grandchildren have probably forgotten them by now. All that remains is the hallowed earth on which they trod and are buried.

Graveyards are one of those things that people either see beauty in or do not. There is something compelling to the author about them. With each visit to the Kalaupapa Peninsula, the road he followed always seemed to lead back to the cemetery with its silent gravestones and untold stories. Some final resting places were not even in the confines of a graveyard and lay so forgotten that never a sprig of foliage or flower petal was placed upon them. These could only be reached by navigating through dense, overgrown thickets. When found, a number were still intact, with stone markers or rectangles made of rocks, while others were bare of any signs except depressions where the earth had sunk a foot or so. In still other places, only a fragment of a broken headstone would be found all by itself. As space allowed there might be a letter or two left to read of the words that were once carved on its whole, but nothing else.

Confucius rightly said so many centuries ago: "Everything has its beauty, but not everyone sees it." The following portion of *The Lands of Father Damien* was created with respect and consolation that Kalaupapa's living, as well as those who lie in these marked and unmarked graves, will be remembered, if nowhere else, through the pages of this book. Each and every one of them had lives, plans and many a tale we will never know. Entitled "Stories Carved In Stone," this chapter is dedicated not only to the peninsula's unknown and forgotten, but to those who still walk upon its ground, and echo to the world all of their untold stories. I believe they would like their book to end this way....

"Our name shall be forgotten in time, and no man shall have our works in remembrance, and our life shall pass away as the trace of a cloud and shall be dispersed as a mist that is driven away with the beams of the sun." AN OLD SONGSTER, BOOK OF WISDOM.

Important Dates

1778 The Sandwich Islands discovered by Englishman Captain James Cook.

1792 Commerce between China and The Sandwich Islands begun.

1835 First documented case of leprosy recorded on the Island of Kauai.

1838 Mother Marianne born as Barbara Cope, January 23, Germany.

1840 Father Damien born as Joseph deVeuster January 3, Belgium.

1843 Brother Joseph Dutton born as Ira. F. Dutton, April 27, Vermont.

1848 First documented case of leprosy reported on the Island of Oahu.

1859 Joseph deVeuster joined the Sacred Hearts Congregation in Belgium.

1863 Leprosy officially recognized as a serious problem in the Islands.

1864 Brother Damien arrived at Honolulu, Oahu, March 19.

1864 Brother Damien ordained a Roman Catholic priest, Honolulu, May 21.

1865 "The Act To Prevent The Spread Of Leprosy" became law, January 3.

1866 First leprosy cases arrived at Kalawao, Molokai, January 6.

1872 Brother Bertrand built St. Philomena Chapel at Kalawao.

1873 Dr. Gerhard Hansen of Norway identified the leprosy bacillus, February 28.

1873 Father Damien arrived on Molokai's Kalaupapa Peninsula, May 10.

1874 Damien built Our Lady of Sorrows Catholic Church, Topside Molokai.

1876 Damien built St. Joseph's Catholic Church, Topside Molokai.

1876 Damien built the first addition to St. Philomena Chapel, Kalawao.

1881 Queen Liliuokalani made a royal visit to the Kalaupapa Peninsula.

1883 Mother Marianne and her Sisters arrived in Honolulu, November 8.

1884 Dr. Arthur Mouritz arrived as the first resident physician at Kalawao.

1885 Damien's leprosy confirmed by Dr. Edward Arning.

1885 Damien established the children's orphanage, Kalawao.

1886 Layman Joseph Dutton arrived at Kalawao, Molokai.

1888 Mother Marianne and two Sisters arrived at Kalaupapa.

1888 Father Conrardy arrived at Kalawao; Father Moellers arrived at Kalaupapa.

1888 Damien began second and last addition to St. Philomena Church.

1889 Father Damien died from leprosy at age 49, Kalawao, April 15.

1890 Population shift from Kalawao to Kalaupapa begun.

1909 U. S. Leprosy Investigation Station opened, Kalawao .

1913 U. S. Leprosy Investigation Station closed, Kalawao.

1918 Mother Marianne died at age 80, buried at Kalaupapa.

1931 Brother Joseph Dutton died at age 88, buried at Kalawao.

1932 Original Baldwin Home closed. Population shift to Kalaupapa completed.

1936 Father Damien remains returned to Belgium.

1947 Sulfone drug treatment introduced for leprosy patients.

1969 Isolation ban for leprosy lifted; last patient admitted to Kalaupapa.

1977 Damien declared "venerable" by Pope Paul VI, the first step toward sainthood.

1980 Kalaupapa National Park officially established.

1981 Hansen's Disease replaced the terminology for leprosy in Hawaii.

1988 Complete restoration of St. Philomena Church.

1995 Damien's beatification by Pope John Paul II, the second step toward sainthood.

1995 The relic of Blessed Damien reinterred at Kalawao, July 22.

Bibliography

Beevers, John. *A Man for Now; The Life of Damien de Veuster, Friend of Lepers.* Doubleday, New York, 1973.

Betz, Eva K. *Yankee at Molokai.* St. Anthony Guild Press, Paterson, New Jersey, 1960.

Cahill, Emmett. *Yesterday at Kalaupapa.* Editions Limited, Honolulu, 1990.

Cauldwell, Irene. *Damien, The Leper Saint.* Camelot Press Ltd., London, 1932.

Cicognani, The Most Reverend Amleto Giovanni, *Father Damien, Apostle of the Lepers.* Washington 1937.

Compton, Piers. *Father Damien.* Alexander Dusely, Ltd., London, 1933.

Daws, Gavan. *Holy Man: Father Damien of Molokai.* University of Hawaii Press, Honolulu, 1984.

Damon, Ethel M. *Siloama: The Church of the Healing Spring.* The Hawaiian Board of Missions. Honolulu, 1948.

Dutton, Charles J. *The Samaritans of Molokai.* Books for Libraries Press, New York, 1932.

Farrow, John. *Damien, the Leper.* Sheed & Ward Inc., New York, 1937.

Gibson, Emma Warren. *Under the Cliffs of Molokai.* Academy Library Guild, Fresno, California, 1957.

Greene, Linda W. *Exile in Paradise: The Isolation of Hawaii's Leprosy Victims and Development of Kalaupapa Settlement, 1865 To The Present.* U.S. Department of the Interior, Denver Service Center, Colorado, 1985.

Hanks, Geoffrey. *Island of no Return-The Story of Father Damien of Molokai.* Pergamon Press, Oxford, England, 1978.

Hanley, Sister Mary Laurence & O. A. Bushnell. *Pilgrimage & Exile: Mother Marianne of Molokai.* University of Hawaii Press, Honolulu, 1991.

Hawaiian Journal of History, Helen G. Chapin, Editor. Volume 21, 1987 and Volume 23, 1989; published by the Hawaiian Historical Society.

Jourdain, Vital SS. CC. Translated from French by Rev. Francis Larkin, SS. CC. and Charles Davenport. *The Heart of Father Damien.* Bruce Publishing Co., Milwaukee, Wisconsin, 1955.

Law, Anwei V. Skinsnes & Wisniewski, Richard A. *Kalaupapa and the Legacy of Father Damien.* Pacific Basin Enterprises, Honolulu, HI. 1988.

Milsome, John. *Damien, Father to the Leper.* Servant Publications, Ann Arbor, Michigan, 1989.

Mouritz, Arthur. *The Path of the Destroyer: A History of Leprosy in the Hawaiian Islands and Thirty Years Research into the Means by Which It Has Spread:* Honolulu Star-Bulletin Ltd, Honolulu, 1916.

Stoddard, Charles Warren. *The Lepers of Molokai.* The Ave Maria Press, Notre Dame, Indiana, 1884.

Summers, Catherine C. *Molokai: A Site Survey.* Bishop Museum, Honolulu, 1971.

Archives, Libraries and Newspapers:

Damien Museum & Archives; Hawaii State Archives; Kalaupapa Archives; Hawaii State Libraries; Honolulu Advertiser; Honolulu Star-Bulletin; Hawaii Catholic Herald; Universal Living Rosary Association of St. Philomena.